Nationwide A<

HIGHER GROUND
AND AWAKENING THE SPIRIT WITHIN

"Very seldom does a young man sit down to write such a compelling account of his Faith journey. All student athletes, indeed all students will benefit from the candor and sincerity Miguel displays in this book."

- *Bill Curry, Former Head Football Coach*
  University of Kentucky

"I feel that this is exactly what our young student athletes need in this day and time. It provides natural and spiritual insight of what a high school football player deals with when making the transition from high school to the college level, not only on the field, but off the field as well. This book should be required reading for all incoming freshmen football players on every college campus in the country."

- *Johnny Shelton, Area Director*
  Central North Carolina FCA
  Free Safety, Atlanta Falcons (1988)

"Student athletes have long needed a book that speaks to the dynamics of their high school and pre-college experiences, one that can help them identify with the pressures and temptations of all sports. Miguel Viera's first person account of such a life has much to offer to those who are truly searching for purpose and direction in lives immersed within the world of student sports."

- *Dr. Pat Cronin, Pastor*
  Friendly Avenue Baptist Church
  Greensboro, N.C.

"If you want to experience major college Football, and Life, from an athlete's perspective, and get the TOTAL picture, Miguel Viera delivers it. This is a special young man, with a special message. I highly recommend this book."

- *Rob Oviatt, Assistant AD, Physical Development*
  Washington State University Athletics

"Walking on Higher Ground and Awakening the Spirit Within was a terrific and enlightening story of a Christian student athlete's life. Each chapter built on each other like scenes from the movie "Hoosiers." I recommend this book to all families, especially those that have aspiring student athletes in their lives."

- *Lee Pena Jr., International Treasury Manager*
  The Sherwin-Williams Company
  Cleveland, Ohio

WALKING ON
HIGHER GROUND
AND AWAKENING THE SPIRIT WITHIN

Walking on Higher Ground and Awakening the Spirit Within
© Copyright 2006 Miguel R. Viera.
All rights reserved. No part of this publication may be reproduced, stored in a retrieval system, or transmitted, in any form or by any means, electronic, mechanical, photocopying, recording, or otherwise, without the written prior permission of the author, except as provided by USA copyright law.

All scripture quotations, unless otherwise indicated, are taken from the New King James Version ®. Copyright © 1979, 1980, 1982, 1988 by Thomas Nelson, Inc. Used by permission. All rights reserved.
© 2006 Parade Publications. All rights reserved
Cover Design: Rachel Viera
Cover Photos: Pamela Viera
Editing: Dr. Doris Henderson

Note for Librarians: A cataloguing record for this book is available from Library and Archives Canada at www.collectionscanada.ca/amicus/index-e.html
ISBN 1-4120-8619-1

Printed in Victoria, BC, Canada. Printed on paper with minimum 30% recycled fibre.
Trafford's print shop runs on "green energy" from solar, wind and other environmentally-friendly power sources.

Offices in Canada, USA, Ireland and UK

Book sales for North America and international:
Trafford Publishing, 6E–2333 Government St.,
Victoria, BC V8T 4P4 CANADA
phone 250 383 6864 (toll-free 1 888 232 4444)
fax 250 383 6804; email to orders@trafford.com
Book sales in Europe:
Trafford Publishing (UK) Limited, 9 Park End Street, 2nd Floor
Oxford, UK OX1 1HH UNITED KINGDOM
phone 44 (0)1865 722 113 (local rate 0845 230 9601)
facsimile 44 (0)1865 722 868; info.uk@trafford.com
Order online at:
trafford.com/06-0375

10 9 8 7 6 5 4 3 2

WALKING ON HIGHER GROUND AND AWAKENING THE SPIRIT WITHIN

*A Christian Student Athlete's
Spiritual Journey
Through the Doors of College
and Beyond*

MIGUEL R. VIERA

CONTENTS

Acknowledgements	9
Introduction	11
Chapter 1 - The Dream of a Young Child	13
Chapter 2 - The Anticipated Recruiting Process	27
Chapter 3 - First Semester at College	45
Chapter 4 - Juggling Academics, Athletics and a Social Life	63
Chapter 5 - The Biggest Decision You'll Ever Make	83
Chapter 6 - Should I Stay, or Should I Go?	103
Chapter 7 - You're Only as Good as You Think You Are	121
Chapter 8 - Life Beyond College Athletics	143
Notes	163
About the Author	167

ACKNOWLEDGEMENTS

I'm most gracious to my Heavenly Father for not only inspiring me to write this book but also giving me the opportunity to spread the gospel. It is an honor and privilege to have Jesus working in my life and continuing to develop my spiritual potential. Without Him, I would be lost.

To my beautiful and caring wife, Tiffany, you have been my everything from day one and everyday just keeps getting better. God has truly blessed me with an angel that I will cherish forever. Your support and encouragement are second to none. You are a wonderful mother and my best friend who without a doubt has the coldest hands and feet this side of the Mason-Dixie Line.

To my son, Mason, watching you grow up has been a blessing and has motivated me to make a difference for the younger generation. Your constant energy, love and bright smiles remind me of how God wants us to come to Him with a childlike faith and excitement.

To my mother, father and brother, Ricardo, for your strong support and encouragement throughout my high school and collegiate football career. I count myself very fortunate to have been raised in such a loving family.

To Ron and Sandy Milner, for giving me your daughter's hand in marriage and welcoming me into your family with open arms. Thanks for all your love and support.

To Coach Bob Lake, your love and enthusiasm for high school football was contagious. Thank you for all the hard work you did sending out game film to colleges and giving me the best possible chance of getting a full scholarship in college football.

To the late Coach Ray Dorr, your constant encouragement and love for your recruits made committing to Kentucky a decision I have never regretted. You will be missed but never forgotten.

To Coach Bill Curry, you taught me how to relate football to life, and it has helped mold me into the person I am today. You were the wisest coach I have ever had and your commitment to academic excellence changed countless lives off the football field.

To Bob Bradley, you took me under your wing at Kentucky and made time in your hectic schedule to be my mentor. I will always cherish the sit-down discussions we had about academics and finances in your office.

To Pastor Pat Cronin, you are certainly a person I aspire to be more like as I grow closer to God. Your powerful sermons on God's word inspire me every week to reach out farther to the lost world. You are not only a good friend but also my spiritual mentor.

To Dr. Doris Henderson, the light of the Lord shines in all you do at Friendly Avenue Baptist Church. You welcomed Tiffany and me with open arms when we first attended FABC, and five years later you are still a dear friend. Thank you for doing a fantastic job editing my book.

To Chris Williams, you inspired me to pursue a full scholarship in college football and took the time to be nice to a small child. If there were more role models like you, this world would be a better place.

A special thanks to Bob Lake, Pastor Pat Cronin, Dr. Doris Henderson, Bill Curry, Johnny Shelton, Lee Pena Jr., Rob Oviatt, Joe Federspiel, Tiffany Viera, Pamela Viera, Donna May, Sandy Milner and Mildred Cox for taking the time to review my book and providing me with your insight and knowledge. You have all played an integral role in helping mold this book into a useful and life-changing story for student athletes, coaches and parents.

INTRODUCTION

As I watch my son Mason (who is now a year old) develop into a young child, I can't help but remember what it was like to be a child myself. At 28 years old of age, I would do just about anything to have a tenth of the energy that my little son burns up throughout the day. To think of the challenges and unlimited opportunities that he will encounter as he grows into a young man has made me realize the importance of writing this book. Who will his role model be when he gets older? It could be one of you reading this book right now. There needs to be an awakening among student athletes that they are role models for our younger generation. Whether you like it or not, the life of a student athlete is scrutinized more closely than that of a non-athletic student.

My Pastor says, "There comes a time in a person's life where he or she wants to give something back to society instead of continuing to take for themselves." As we move farther into the 21st century, high schools and colleges struggle with having real student athletes who achieve their potential and serve as good role models for the younger generation. It seems that somewhere between the 1990's and 2000's, there was a disconnect between the student/athlete and teacher/coach relationship. That ill-fated day at Columbine High School in Littleton, Colorado, that claimed fifteen lives shows the significant importance of good role models in our society. It seems that student athletes often forget that their teachers and coaches are there to help them achieve and succeed.

I find it ironic that the negative shift in this country's role models coincides with our society continuing to find ways to take God out of the public schools, not to mention high school football. They say it is being done so no one gets offended, but it is offensive to me that the minority of this country are making decisions for the majority. The reason our country stands apart from any other place on this planet is because our founding fathers knew the importance of the central role that God should play in the United States of America. I emphasize the words "central role" because as we move farther and farther into the 21st century, we have seen the Ten Commandments taken out of the public schools and Christmas in our country has suddenly turned into Happy Holidays.

WALKING ON HIGHER GROUND AND AWAKENING THE SPIRIT WITHIN

Did you know that on June 19, 2000, the Supreme Court ruled in favor of a vote of 6-3 to ban team prayers led by coaches before high school football games? Some of my most memorable moments during high school football were during the Lord's Prayer before our Friday night games. It is a shame that high school football players across the country will never have the opportunity to be led in prayer by their respective coaches. I highly encourage student athletes to initiate prayer in the locker room, which is not against the law. The experience of witnessing the power and awe of God filling a locker room with His spirit, while His prayer is spoken with knees bent, heads bowed, and eyes shut is what made playing the game of football so special to me.

When is enough going to be enough to where a voice is finally heard in our society for the majority who want God back in public schools and back in the government? The student athletes of tomorrow need to rise above the decline of this country's athletic role models and stand for what is right and just. If we can work together to put God back into high school and college football, we will be a step closer to helping reform our country's core values.

This is a book not only for student athletes at the collegiate level but also for high school students who are involved in athletics and are preparing to go to college. Parents, teachers and coaches are also encouraged to read this book to better help understand the mind of an athletic teenager. Life is too short for students to experience everything, so I'm hoping that through this book, you'll be able to avoid the pitfalls of college and reap all the rewards that experience has to offer. The student athlete life is very demanding, and there are strong pressures to take shortcuts to achieve optimal results. I've seen too many athletes at the collegiate level take the road more traveled, which has resulted in their sitting in far too much traffic. We'll discuss how to overcome these pressures while achieving your maximum academic and athletic potential, while even more importantly, developing your spiritual life. So sit back, kick off your shoes, and get ready for the ride of your life. For some of you, I can guarantee that reading this book will be a life-changing experience.

CHAPTER ONE

THE DREAM OF A YOUNG CHILD

Good thoughts are no better than good dreams, unless they are executed.
- RALPH WALDO EMERSON

Make no little plans; they have no magic to stir men's blood...Make big plans, aim high in hope and work.
- DANIEL BURNHAM

*A*s a five-year-old boy, besides going to kindergarten, I had nothing to do but play with my brother, Ricardo, and our GI JOE and Star Wars toys all day. Of course, mom would make us take breaks to nourish our little bodies with plenty of food and beverages. I like to think of those as the good old days! Those days were long before raising a family, working 40+ hours a week and paying what seems to be a continuous stream of bills. Those were the days where a child could pretend to be whatever one's wildest dreams would allow. Maybe you were a cowboy in the Wild West, beating up your brother, the Indian. Perhaps you would take an imaginary trip to the moon and back. If you wanted, you could even pretend to be in the Army while rolling on the floor with your plastic gun and jumping on or over the couch. The point is that nothing limited the dream of this little boy.

At an early age, I was fascinated with my father and his love for lifting weights. There is something about big muscles that cry out masculinity to a little boy. To me, the larger-than-life biceps of my father were the coolest things I had ever seen. At the age of five, I started working out with my dad as often as I could. I was not bench-pressing, power-lifting or dead-lifting, but if I had been you would have seen my picture in the Guinness Book of World Records for the youngest power-lifter in the world. No, I was sticking to the basic exercises like pull-ups, push-ups and sit-ups. Even at a young age, there was something about exercising and getting my body to grow that fascinated me. Probably, an important reason for this was that it gave me more leverage against my brother when we got into altercations over who would get to shoot the first rubber band at the plastic army soldiers we set-up in the dining room.

Exercising as a young child quickly became as routine as brushing my teeth and roughing up my brother every chance I got. I have to give my brother a lot of credit. It could not have been easy having me as the older sibling. I remember always completing his sentences as a small child and acting as the official baby gibberish interpreter for my mother. My brother would say something to the effect of goo-goo ga-ga and I would interpret it as Ricardo says he wants me to finish off his macaroni and cheese!

A word of advice to older siblings that are reading this book: Be nice to your younger siblings, because once you are full grown, there is a good chance that they will be taller than you and probably able to kick your butt! Now that my brother is over 6'3 and I am barely pushing 6'3 with my black alligator boots on, which offer some nice artificial elevation, I am nice to him all the time. Regardless of who is taller or older, the reason I want to talk about my brother is because he played a key role in the development of my athletic career. You cannot have a better supporting cast around you than your own family.

As I grew older and my body developed, something happened that has carried on to this day. It was the ultimate discovery of a muscle that others kids and adults wanted to see. All the pull-ups, push-ups and sit-ups started paying off in big dividends. I was flexing my biceps for others just like my dad had flexed his biceps for me. I remember going over my friend Frank's house for sleepovers in the 2nd and 3rd grade. As soon as we stepped into the house, he would say, "Flex your muscles for my mom." There is something special about being put on the spot as a little boy and being able to deliver the goods.

It is funny what things children pick-up from their parents. This goes to show how important it is to have a good influence on your children. Don't think for a second they will not notice something like smoking cigarettes or consuming too much alcohol. Mistakes made raising a child in the early years can be detrimental to their well being and have a long-lasting and damaging effect. I can honestly say since my son, Mason, was born, I have taken on a new appreciation of my parents. You start to reflect on the things you did as a child and wish you could go back in time and behave a little differently.

You can definitely say that I was not your average kid. There was a uniqueness that combined Arnold Swartzenegger's love for exercise, Donald Trump's savvy business skills, and how can I leave out Michael Jackson's "Afro" prior to his success with the Thriller album. Yes, that's right, I said "Afro". I am ashamed to admit now that I was such a huge Michael Jackson fan as a child. I not only had a pretty stellar "Afro," but leather pants and a glove to match. If a poster, calendar, button pin, book or trading card existed that I did not have, it wasn't long before I found it.

I remember the first time I got in trouble at school. The teacher called my mother at home and told her that I wouldn't let a girl look at my Michael Jackson View Master. When my mother asked me why I wouldn't let her see it, I told her she didn't have the 50 cents that I was charging. Not only was I getting an education but also earning a little extra for candy on the side! Did I mention that I mastered the art of origami at an early age? For a shiny nickel or dime kids were lining up on the bus to get paper frogs that hopped, birds that flapped their wings, mouths that talked or even a paper balloon you could blow up with air. That's what I like to call "thinking outside of the box." I remember earning a quarter once for selling a bottle cap full of glue with a toothpick to one of my school friends. I think I told him that it was a sailboat.

Every child is different and unique, and that should be embraced by parents and children alike. It would be a boring world if everyone liked doing the same thing and dressed the same way. As the old saying goes, "variety is the spice of life". Therefore, to a child his limitations should only be limited by his imagination and not by the expectations of others. John Eldredge, in his book "Wild at Heart" says, "Capes and swords, camouflage, bandannas and six-shooters - these are the uniforms of boyhood. Little boys yearn to know they are powerful, they are dangerous, they are someone to be reckoned with." Think of how different the world would be in a good way if children of all ages yearned to know those three things.

As every young child has experienced, being associated with the wrong crowd can turn your world upside down in a hurry. I remember a boy in my childhood named Darryl (not real name), who had that very effect on my life. Darryl had been held back at least two years by the time he reached 4th grade and was known for getting into trouble. When we rode the bus to school, it was not unusual for Darryl to sneak beer onto the back of the bus and then urinate on the radiator. He was just the type of kid your parents do not want to be your friend.

I think, especially for boys, there is some invisible force that has the tendency to drive us down the wrong road at times even with our better judgment at hand. As I started to hang out with Darryl more, my grades started dropping; my attitude toward my parents and brother quickly changed; and I really was becoming the person that I feared the most. That person was someone who was interfering with my dreams and aspirations. Sure, I was only nine years old, but I knew then that there was something bigger than myself to be achieved. It could be within my grasp in the future, if I stayed on the right road. Of course, at the time, I did not know what that thing was, but I could feel it with all my heart, which made it real.

As a child there comes a point where the only person who can make a decision to rescue you in the type of situation that I was in is yourself, and not your parents. Sure, my parents were concerned and tried talking to me about my changes in behavior, but it was ultimately my own decision that opted to end my friendship with Darryl and pursue my dreams. Parents can only guide and instruct their children on how to live their lives to their fullest, but it is the child who has to make the decision as to which road to follow. Making the decision to become a leader and not a follower that day was definitely a monumental turning point in my life.

THE NEED FOR PHYSICAL CONTACT

When I was in the fourth grade and fully equipped with guns (that is slang for biceps), which by the way were outlawed in 48 states, something new caught my eye. I think it is fair to say that whether you are a young boy or girl, there is one fun thing to do that is pretty much universal. That one thing is running into stationary or moving objects as fast as you can and falling down. Football gave me the permission to do that on a frequent basis.

Just the other day for my son's one-year birthday party, I was watching our neighbor's son from across the street running down our hill in the backyard. At 28 years old, if I were running down that hill there would either have to be an emergency in the house, or it was time to eat dinner, because I'm a real big fan of food. The little boy simply ran as fast as he could down the hill and just tumbled on the ground. That is one of the great things about children, they do not over-think what they are going to do; they just live for the moment.

It was at a Catholic school called Annunciation in Cleveland, Ohio, that my football career began as a young child. I had the license to tackle other kids my age and instead of getting yelled at, I would get a pat on the back. I was not the type of kid that needed to touch the ball and score touchdowns; I was content keeping things simple. When you are on the defense, you do not have to worry about any fancy trick plays. You simply find the kid that has the football and tackle him in a hurry.

WALKING ON HIGHER GROUND AND AWAKENING THE SPIRIT WITHIN

During my kindergarten year at Annunciation there was an older kid in seventh grade who has had a lasting effect on my life even to this day. His name was Chris Williams, and he was the best running back that this little boy had ever seen. There was something about having Chris as a role model in my life that was electric and exciting. It felt like I was bigger, stronger and faster because of it, even though my baby teeth were still coming in. Chris would take the time to say "hello" to me and talk to me around his friends. We even went on a field trip to the Cleveland Zoo, and Chris was my chaperone.

Annunciation only went to the eighth grade, and Chris received a full scholarship to St. Edwards Catholic High School on the other side of town. Although I did not get to see him at school, he kept in touch with me, and when he was playing high school football, my mom would get tickets so we could go to his games. I remember watching one of his games in November of his senior year. He must have rushed for what seemed to be over 250 yards that night under those Friday night football lights. Besides Chris's outstanding performance on the field, this was a memorable game, because that frigid November Cleveland night was one of the coldest I had experienced. It was so cold that we used our garbage bags full of shredded paper to keep our feet warm.

The next thing that happened was one of the greatest gifts that could have ever been given to a small child. After St. Edwards narrowly lost to their rivals, my mother, brother and I walked alongside the turf football field to catch a glimpse of Chris. Just at that moment, he caught me in the corner of his eye and waved me over to come onto the football field. I hesitated for a second, wanting to turn around to see if he was waving at someone else, but to my childish disbelief, he was calling me over to say "hello." Getting to step onto that turf football field that night and stand amongst those heroic football players meant the world to me!

Chris is an example of the real role models our society is longing to rediscover. We need role models who are unselfish and willing to do something as small as speaking to a child and offering a friendly word of encouragement. Those acts of kindness started me well on my way to becoming a better person, as well as a better football player. I will always be grateful to Chris Williams for opening my eyes to football and for his kind heart toward a small child. I remember the night that Chris was on the ten o'clock news and signed his letter of intent to attend NC

State University and receive a full scholarship to play football for the Wolfpack. Even as a small child, I knew that was a goal that I was more than willing to pursue.

I truly believe that the good Lord has made all of us different and unique. As small children, we are drawn to different types of athletic activities. For one boy, it might be playing basketball with his friends, while another enjoys the thrill of tee ball. A small girl might grow up with a love for volleyball, while her sister excels at softball. I feel truly blessed that as I started football and enjoyed the sport as a child, my parents were always there to encourage and provide for me. There are fewer things more tragic than a child who has to grow up in an abusive home or in a poverty-stricken family. It is hard enough for a child to simply try to fit in at school, get good grades, excel at sports, play an instrument or have to kiss Aunt Jewel on the cheek every time she is at a family gathering.

Football was an excellent outlet to dispense my energy. The great thing about it was I did not care who won or lost the game. I was just happy to be part of a team and of course, get to tackle the opponent. One unforeseeable benefit to many outside the arena of this great sport was getting the opportunity to get scabs! This might seem strange to the reader, but nothing goes better with muscles than a cool looking scar, regardless of how small. A scab to a child or even to this 28-year-old writer is a delightful and irresistible thing to pick.

One of the things about the 21st century that I think is a shame is the number of children whose parents have them on tranquilizing drugs because they supposedly have too much energy. I am not saying that there are not children who have serious medical problems that need to be medically treated; however, I wonder if fewer children would need these drugs if their parents would get them away from the television and outside to play. Yes, I think this has gone on long enough and someone needs to stop pointing fingers at the children and start pointing them at the parents. In Lionel Tigers' book "The Decline of Males", he says,

> *At least three to four times as many boys than girls are essentially defined as ill because their preferred patterns of play don't fit easily into the structure of the school. Well-meaning psycho-managers then prescribe tranquilizing drugs for ADD, such as Ritalin...The situation is scandalous.*

> The use of drugs so disproportionately among boys betrays the failure of school authorities to understand sex differences...The disease these boys may have is being male.

Even though this author seems to be blaming the school system for the increase in Ritalin use, the parents are the one's authorizing the use of such medication. Let's face it; raising a child in our society is a huge responsibility. More parents have to step up to the plate and stop letting societal influences (such as television programs, vulgar music and graphic video games) raise their children. The movie "The Cable Guy," starring Jim Carrey, is an excellent example of how many children are being raised this way in the United States. Jim Carrey's character is shown as a child sitting in front of the television for countless hours' everyday while his parents give him no attention. This leads to the character growing up without any friends and contributes to a long list of violations with the law, not to mention a fixation for illegally installing cable to make friends.

In a recent article in Parade magazine called "We Need to Pay More Attention to Boys", the First Lady, Laura Bush, has chosen to spend the next four years in the White House to encourage and find better ways for parents/coaches/role models to be mentors for boys. What better way for a student athlete to have a positive effect on our society. She is quoted in the article as saying,

> I think we need to pay more attention to boys. I think we've paid a lot of attention to girls for the last 30 years, and we have this idea in the United States that boys can take care of themselves. We've raised them to be totally self-reliant, starting really too early. They need the nurturing that all humans need. And I think there are a lot of life skills that we teach girls but don't teach boys. We actually have neglected boys.

The article goes on to talk about how boys' attendance rates in college have declined in comparison to girls and how they are the ones causing trouble, dropping out of school and getting involved with drugs and alcohol. She feels there are a great deal of families that are staying focused on teaching good values, but states, "I'm not so sure our big national media is a partner in it." The First Lady then adds, "People have the power. They have the television knob. They can turn it off." This last part is something I think all parents need to be more mindful of regarding their children. She says, "In some ways, I think today we have to protect our children from society, rather than raise children to fit into society. We should want them to not be exactly like everything they see on TV or in the movies or listen to in music."

Fortunately, for my brother and me, our parents were in the construction business and not members of the demolition crew. Their encouraging words were fuel for the fire that burned inside this little boy's heart to be the best I could be at football. It is funny and reminiscent reflecting back as a child and remembering my first couple years of football. One thing that will always be fresh in my mind was when I had to undergo my first surgery. No, I didn't break an arm or leg playing football but I did have to get my tonsils removed. When I first started playing football, my tonsils would swell up to the size of golf balls in the back of my throat, making it hard to get any air into my oxygen-depleted lungs.

There are three undeniably cool things about getting this surgery as a child. The first is that you can only eat Popsicles for the first couple of days, which is like a free ticket to Sugar Town. Secondly, I got to relax away from school and watch nothing but movies. Thirdly and most importantly, the doctor was kind enough to let me keep my tonsils in a jar full of formaldehyde. This proved to be a big hit with the kids at school during "Show and Tell" time. I'm not quite sure if modern medicine would allow bringing home tonsils today, but there was definitely a sense of accomplishment getting to bring home that prize after surgery. There was definitely a high gross factor, but to a kid, that is what made it so special. Just so you know, I didn't charge anyone to see my tonsils; however, looking back, that would have been a great idea.

CORNFIELDS, COWS AND OPEN LAND

It was in the middle of the sixth grade that my parents made the decision to leave the Cleveland area and move out to the country in Medina, OH. A main reason for this was because of the condition of the Cleveland public schools at the time and my parents' fear that my brother and I would have to go to different high schools. This proved to be a wise move. There was a deep longing for two brothers to breathe in and embrace everything the country life had to offer.

The dream of every little boy is to have unlimited space for roaming and playing, and that is just what two and a half acres in the country had to offer. Right next door was a half-acre pond that was stocked with bass. If you combined that with our property sitting right next to a wooded area, you had the next best thing to Disney World. One of the first things I did was to build a two-story tree house where my brother and I could set up our fort. The country life proved to be all it promised. We had chickens, ducks, rabbits, a dog and what must have been a dozen cats from a recent litter.

By the time I reached the age of thirteen, I started lifting free weights, and that is when my body really started growing. My brother started to exercise with me at times. With nothing but a full garage of weight equipment, there was no excuse for not working out on a frequent basis. I often had friends come over and showed them how to do different exercises.

The transition to a different school was fortunately easy for us due to the country lifestyle. In the township where we lived (Lafayette), instead of worrying about getting your house robbed, one was more likely to ask, "Is my house going to get toilet-papered?" or "Is someone going to go cow-tipping again with farmer John's cows?"

It is funny how kids have different nicknames growing up in school. Luckily, for me, the hit TV show "Saved by the Bell" was very popular at the time. Thanks to that show, my fellow classmates gave me the nickname of AC Slater. It helped that I had that Puerto Rican olive skin, muscular arms, curly black hair and a few dimples like AC when I smiled. Your identity and charm as a child growing up should be embraced. Let me be clear when I say there is no such thing as an average boy or girl but instead, every child is extraordinary. Thankfully, the "Afro" was long gone by the time I reached the eighth grade. Otherwise, I could have been called JJ from "Goodtimes."

The eight grade at Cloverleaf Junior High was an experimental time for me with sports. Not only did I play football in the fall, but I wrestled in the winter and tried track and field during the spring. It is important for young student athletes to try their hand at multiple sports to see which ones really ignite their desire to be competitive. Wrestling was a good experience for me. It is a game of balance and strength, and when all is said and done after a match, you and you alone are to be held accountable for your success or failure. That year at the 132-lb weight class, I racked up a record of 13 wins and 2 losses. I still remember those yellow and white safety pins that I attached to my jean jacket every time I pinned an opponent. Those pins on my jacket served as a sense of accomplishment to this young student of the game.

My Grandpa Viera was an avid fan of wrestling when I was in the eighth grade, but a different kind of wrestling. He was an old school fan of Hulk Hogan, Big John Stud, Andre the Giant and the legendary Jimmy "The Super Fly" Snooka. When we used to go to his house to visit and whenever I told him I was wrestling, he had this crazy idea that I meant "professional" wrestling. My Grandpa was from Puerto Rico and although his English was limited, I tried to explain to him the difference between the two. After many unsuccessful attempts, I figured if he wanted to think I was a professional wrestler in the eighth grade, then "no harm no foul."

Track and Field did not really catch much of my attention. Sure, I tried doing the shot put, discus throw and running different events on the track, but these activities just did not offer the same kind of thrill as football. Running at someone full speed and leaping on them like an African Lion pouncing on its prey in the Safari was a sport that could not be matched by any other! I decided then that I would only pursue football and train year round to develop my potential in order to take a step closer to achieving what my friend, Chris Williams, had accomplished. The goal was a full paid scholarship to a Division I football program.

By the time I reached the ninth grade I was tipping the scales at about 145 lbs. I looked at my body as a mold of clay that could be sculpted and built into something great like the former bodybuilder Arnold Swartzenegger. Freshman year in high school was also when grades started to count towards my GPA. That was something I took very seriously and made every effort to excel in all of my classes, in addition to excelling on the football field. Through hard work and dedication to my studies I finished the year with above a 3.9 GPA. In addition, I already had caught the eye of the head football coach at Cloverleaf High School through my aggressive style of play at the linebacker position. I had also been named most valuable defensive player for the team.

There are some things in life that are not going to be the most enjoyable things to do, but they are necessary. Doing the right thing among some circles of friends might not be viewed as popular. Sure, I knew kids who did not take school seriously and did what they had to do to get by. My perspective in life has always been if you are going to do something halfway, there is no point even starting it. Let's face it: There are countless things that are more enjoyable than studying for upcoming tests, consistently attending classes and paying attention through taking notes in class. But if you want to be successful in life, these things are necessary. When you see the big picture that your teachers and parents are trying to communicate to you, it is easier to focus your energy in the right areas of your life, because you know the potential outcome of all your hard work.

THE ULTIMATE LIP SYNCH CONTEST

The last thing I want to do is give the impression that during my freshman year of high school I did not have any fun. One fun, memorable and defining moment in the ninth grade that lived with me throughout my high school experience was a lip synch contest I entered during our ninth grade dance. Back in the early 90's there was a new song that was quickly rising up the charts. I knew from the first time I heard it that this song had it all. It was cool, hip and half of the song was in Spanish, which gave it an exotic flare. Most importantly, it was a big hit with the ladies. That song was called "Rico Suave". I remember watching the video for the song, and something inside me just screamed out that I had to do this song for the lip synch contest. For the next month leading up to the contest, I memorized "Rico Suave", assembled the finest crew of air guitarists that Cloverleaf Junior High had to offer, recruited two young ladies as dancers, choreographed dance moves and of course, arranged for the costumes.

One reason this song motivated me is because it embraced my father's culture and part of who I am. Back on January 24, 1954, my father, Leonardo Lee Viera was born in a small town in Puerto Rico called

Quebradillas. He was one of six children born to John and Pilar Viera. At a very young age, my father's family moved to Cleveland, Ohio, due to my Grandpa Viera winning the state lottery. He moved his entire family, so he could work in a steel factory with a friend of the family. If this course of events had never taken place, I would not be writing this book today. I have always embraced being Puerto Rican, and this song for me was a way to show others a part of my ethnicity that they had never seen.

I can still remember getting ready behind stage to face the seventh, eighth and ninth grade crowd for the lip synch contest. Sure, there were butterflies in this fifteen-year-old's stomach, but there was also an excitement and thrill of the unknown that urged me to move forward. My three air guitarists had real guitars that they were going to pretend to play. The two dancers had matching outfits, and were ready to dance by my side. I was dressed for the part on that cool country spring night. There was a bandana around my head, a fake earring on my left ear, an unzipped brown leather jacket that covered my shoulders, back and arms, but couldn't hide my newly discovered abs and chest that were covered with a light layer of baby oil. Throw in a tight fitting pair of jeans and black cowboy boots, and there was a real live Spanish cowboy getting ready to rock the crowd.

The moment I stepped onto the stage to lip synch "Rico Suave", the gymnasium air was filled with screams of approval. The music started, and I began to lip synch and dance like I had never danced before. My three air guitarists were moving to the music and playing air guitars like they were members of a rock band; the two dancers were dancing to the rhythm of Spanish music; and I was working the crowd beyond what I ever could have imagined. Every time I pulled down my brown leather jacket a little bit, the screams and shrieks from the crowd would only grow louder. Once the song was complete and the performance had ended, I knew that this was a moment in my life that I would never forget.

That night our group placed second in the contest behind three ninth grade boys who dressed up as women and sang Aretha Franklin's "R-E-S-P-E-C-T." Although the crowd favorite that night was "Rico Suave", the teachers were the judges and not the students. It was bitter defeat for this fifteen-year-old boy, but I was proud of taking the bold step forward to do something different in my life. That night there was certainly a risk of not being accepted by the crowd and also the uncertainty of whether my group's performance would be successful or a complete failure in the eyes of the judges. However, those were risks I was willing to take. You see, a leader is someone who is willing to take a risk to reap a greater reward. I was quickly becoming a leader instead of a follower and got to embrace my Puerto Rican ethnicity in the process. Up to the year I graduated from Cloverleaf High School, friends and even students I didn't know would come up to me and say, "Remember when you did "Rico Suave" in the ninth grade lip synch contest?" I would just smile and say, "I sure do."

CHAPTER TWO

THE ANTICPATED RECRUITING PROCESS

There are many plans in a man's heart, Nevertheless the Lord's counsel - that will stand.
- PROVERBS 19:21

Be anxious for nothing, but in everything by prayer and supplication, with thanksgiving, let your requests be made known to God; and the peace of God, which surpasses all understanding, will guard your heart and minds through Christ Jesus.
- PHILIPPIANS 4:6-7

WALKING ON HIGHER GROUND AND AWAKENING THE SPIRIT WITHIN

The 10th grade at Cloverleaf High School was different from most other schools. Due to our small school, 10th through 12th grade was in a separate building from the Junior High, which was composed of the 7th through 9th graders. The reason I mention this is because as I entered the 10th grade, it was like starting at a different school all over again with new students and teachers. The summer of 1991 was a large step toward achieving the goal of earning a full scholarship in football. Ever since I saw my childhood hero, Chris Williams, sign that letter of intent on television to play football at NC State University, I knew my dream was getting closer everyday.

There was a great deal of anticipation and excitement leading up to my sophomore football year. Thinking of being able to play under those Friday night football lights amid stands packed with thousands of screaming fans was just the motivation I needed to prepare for the upcoming football season. Through a consistent off-season training program that consisted of lifting weights four times a week, running three times a week and eating everything in sight, I tipped the scales at about 160 lbs when I reported for two-a-day football practices. Although practices initially started out well, a tackling drill that I participated in resulted in breaking my ring finger on my left hand. This was an injury that I received a lot of slack for from the players. Many of them felt that if you break a finger you should just tape it up and get back in the game. I guess you can say I was dealing with a tough crowd. Due to the severity of the break, the only way for it to heal properly was for me to get a cast put on my left hand that pulled the ring finger down. This resulted in missing more than half of the 2001 football season. Once the break had healed, I was given the green light to play football again.

Although I had been a linebacker my whole life (except for a short-lived career as running back in the seventh grade) my head coach, Bob Lake, saw something special in me as a player. He decided to start me at nose tackle for the remaining four games of the year on the varsity squad. I can still remember the first high school tackle I made against the North Royalton Golden Bears and hearing my name called out by the announcer. It still echoes in my memory as he said, "That was number 40, Miguel Viera, on the tackle." My name was not pronounced correctly on that night, but one thing was for sure, and that was that he said my name. Hearing my name being called over those speakers on Friday nights was something that I got accustomed to hearing as my high school football career progressed.

Even though I was undersized for the defensive line, I learned to utilize my speed to outsmart my opponents. On many occasions, not soon after the ball was snapped, I would squeeze between the offensive linemen and wreak havoc in the backfield. I quickly learned that the bigger the linemen were, the harder they would fall. One of my favorite positions to be in was when we were defending our goal and the defensive linemen would assume the position called "root hog." Plain and simple, this was getting as low to the ground as possible so when the ball snapped, you would just lunge at the ankles of the offensive lineman in front of you. This strategy cleared out the first layer of the offense and allowed the linebackers and secondary to play clean up with whoever was carrying the football.

My first varsity game resulted in another fond memory. It was second down and goal, and the opposing team's offense was intent on pushing our defense against our goal and threatening to score. Something had to be done quickly by our eleven defensive players. Someone had to step up and make a play. At the snap of the ball, I made myself skinny, which was not difficult to do at 160 lbs. I proceeded to torpedo towards the running back almost before he was even given the football. After a loud smashing blow to the ball carrier, something felt very strange. As I hit the running back, there was an awkward sensation in my left arm. As a matter of fact, I could not feel my left arm at all. It appeared that somehow my funny bone was triggered, which resulted in playing the remainder of the drive with what felt like a limp spaghetti noodle hanging from my shoulder. That hit in my eyes was viewed as my initiation into high school football. The fact that I stayed out there and continued to play proved that I was not only born to play this great game but capable of doing great things on the football field.

I was only able to play in four varsity games in my sophomore football season of 1991 but the stage was being set for greater things to come. That year I not only lettered in football as a sophomore but also was named one of two most outstanding sophomore football players. Small steps would soon lead to bigger accomplishments in the near future.

BODYBUILDING 101

Prior to the start of my junior year at Cloverleaf High school, I decided to enter a couple of bodybuilding competitions. I figured that since I was lifting weights and getting ready for the upcoming football season, this would be a good chance to put my muscles into action. My first bodybuilding competition was definitely an interesting experience. Not really understanding all the preparation that was involved in bodybuilding, I signed up for a meet called "The Governor's Cup." The competing age bracket that I fell into was 17 years and under, and now I had another reason to hit the weights besides just football.

There are a few things in life that show a man's physical weaknesses like a pair of black posing trunks. A person might look good in a gym with a pair of shorts and a tank top but like my wife says, "posing trunks leave little to the imagination." I remember when I stood in front of the mirror in my black posing trunks and thought, "I've got some real work to do." The thought of having to stand in front of a large crowd in a small, confined piece of clothing was all the motivation I needed.

After several months of intense training and strict dieting, I just had a couple of things to take care of before I would be ready. There was the matter of shaving my body, tanning and practicing my posing routine. That's right, I said, "shaving my body." Now depending on how much body hair a person has, this could be an all day event with a can of shaving cream and a Bic razor. Luckily, for me, the process was not as bad as it could have been due to being a young teen.

A couple of trips to the tanning bed and some self-applying "Pro Tan" proved to be all I needed due to my olive skin. The posing routine came naturally due to plenty of practice posing as a child; however, there was still the matter of choosing the posing music. This decision came instantaneously, due to my admiration for the bodybuilding legend, Arnold Swartzennegger. The theme song to the movie "Conan the Barbarian" was exactly what best suited this rookie bodybuilder.

The day of the competition finally came, and I was anxious to partake in my first bodybuilding meet. There were a couple of things that had to be completed before stepping out on the stage in front of the audience. The first and probably most important was not to drink too much water that day due to the potential of it hiding the definition in the muscles.

Secondly, it was crucial to have a solid preparatory routine prior to stepping on the stage. This is where contestants would coat themselves with baby oil to better display what bodybuilders call "cuts" and "striations" as they worked out in the "pump up room." I know what you are thinking to yourself, "What in the world is a pump up room?" Don't worry; it isn't as bad as it sounds. The "pump up room" is merely a room full of weight equipment where the bodybuilder can get a final pump to ensure that their muscles are peaking to capacity before stepping onstage.

After completing the backstage preparation, I was chosen to be the first poser to do his routine for my weight class. I'll never forget the feeling of gratification that overcame me as I went through my posing routine onstage. There is something very special about another person applauding an individual's hard work and dedication. After months of intense training for this competition, there I was posing to the theme song to "Conan the Barbarian," while the spectators in the auditorium applauded my efforts. At that moment, it didn't matter whether I won or lost that night. It was more about the respect and admiration of my peers. That night I placed second and got a nice trophy, but more importantly, I started to really understand why it was important to appreciate others around you. Applauding others' efforts fuels their spirits and motivates them to reach higher and farther than they ever could have possibly imagined.

ALMOST THE PERFECT SEASON

There must have been something special in the fall air of 1992. That was the year that put the Cloverleaf High School football team on the map in Ohio. After a disappointing season in 1991 that resulted in a record below .500, there was something to be proved on that football field under those Friday night lights. Doubles started in the humid summer heat of mid-August, and as the team got closer to approaching the first game of the season, everyone was excited to see how the season would unfold. The team was not only loaded with experienced players like our junior quarterback and myself at middle linebacker, but a highly recruited senior running back/linebacker and wide receiver/free safety would prove to be the difference makers in 1992.

WALKING ON HIGHER GROUND AND AWAKENING THE SPIRIT WITHIN

The first game of the year was against the Wadsworth Grizzlies. This was the first game that I started at the middle linebacker position for the Cloverleaf High School football team. Now every football game that has ever been played can be decided by the team which ends the game with more accumulated momentum on their side. These shifts of momentum, in some cases, continuously go back and forth throughout the duration of the game. The 2002 season started with such a play.

The Cloverleaf Colts won the coin toss and decided to kick the ball off to the Wadsworth Grizzlies. There I was on the kickoff team, not knowing how the season would unfold, but knowing that I was going to give nothing less than 100% on every play. As we kicked the ball off, I sprinted as fast as my legs would take me and was focused on the location of the receiver catching and returning the ball. As I dodged blockers on the way to the path of the return specialist, I continued to pick up speed and before I knew it, I was crashing into the ball carrier. The jarring hit propelled the ball out of the receiver's hands and it was a Cloverleaf recovery within the 20-yard line on the opponent's side of the field. That play alone stands out in my mind, because it was not only the first play of the season, but also the play that started the momentum for the 1992 season.

Eight games later the Colts were 8-0 and feeling better than ever. The last undefeated team at Cloverleaf was in 1972 when the team went 10-0. The town was buzzing and the television media was talking about the football team that played amongst the cornfields and cows. You could not ask for a better season, and I even got to do my first television interview with the local news station. Best of all, due to our undefeated record and some excellent senior talent, recruiting coaches from college football programs like Penn State, Indiana, Purdue, Ohio State and Michigan were coming to watch our games.

One of the big games during that season was against the Brunswick Blue Devils. It was a game that was televised in the Cleveland viewing area and there were supposedly recruiters from some big-time college football programs who were going to be in the stands. If I ever had a chance to make a statement as a player during my junior year, this was it. I can still remember Coach Lake coming up to me before the game and letting me know that this was the big one.

Athletes sometimes enter a state of euphoria called the zone when playing their particular sport. You have probably seen this with players like Michael Jordan hitting every shot he takes or Tom Brady completing every pass to his receivers. I can only remember two times I have played football when I was truly in the zone - a place where your focus is razor sharp and your tackling is at its finest. The first time was against the Brunswick Blue Devils, and the second time I will talk about later in the book.

That night in our victory over the Brunswick Blue Devils, I registered 18 tackles. It seemed like I knew where every play was going before the ball was even snapped. Whether it was a run or pass play, I was on it like white on rice. Later that week it was announced to the team that I was named Cleveland Plain Dealer Defensive Player of the Week. This was another giant step to achieving my goal of earning a full scholarship to a college football program.

There is a reason why sailboats can come with an outboard engine. The reason is that the wind does not always blow and fill the sail and eventually you have to use something besides nature to propel your vessel. The wind finally died down in our ninth game against the Berea Braves. They had only one loss in the season and were competing with us for first place in the Pioneer Conference. This was a team that our school had never beaten, which added to the drama. Just like the Florida State Seminoles, their fans did the tomahawk chop in the stands, which annoys me to this day. This was by far the biggest game of the year, and the winner would not only win the Pioneer Conference, but also have an excellent chance of making it to the state playoffs. Our Coach even had players from the 1972 undefeated team come and talk to us before the game to let us know that this was a special moment in our lives and that regardless of what happened, it would never be forgotten.

It was not that the Cloverleaf Colts played bad that night; it was just that we did not play better than the other team. The scores battled back and forth, and the game came down to the last drive for the Colts. I helplessly watched from the sidelines as our perfect season suddenly became a distant memory. The pass thrown by our quarterback was intercepted by one of the opponent's cornerbacks. I remember the feeling of defeat that night as I played my heart out and left everything on the field only to lose 14-22. A magical season came crashing down with a single defeat. We went on to win our final game against our neighboring rivals, the Medina Bees, but the bitter taste of defeat was still in our mouths. We placed second in the Pioneer Conference that year because Berea's loss was against a non-conference team and on top of that a 9-1 record was not enough to get us into the playoffs. Only four teams in our district made it to the playoffs that year and we had accumulated enough points to be the fifth team out. By the way, the 10-0 team in 1972 did not make the playoffs either.

It was still a season to remember, and although it was not perfect, two of our senior players benefited from the excellent season. Our running back/linebacker accepted a full scholarship to Penn State and our receiver/free safety accepted a full scholarship to Kent State that school year. What would the 1993 season hold for the Cloverleaf Colts? With many returning players, including our quarterback and myself at middle linebacker, the small country town of Lodi was expecting big things.

COLLEGE FOOTBALL CAMP BLUES

Now that my junior football season was behind me, I found myself walking with a spring in my step and very focused for the upcoming football season. After receiving most valuable defensive player at the football awards banquet and being named Second Team All-Pioneer Conference, I knew that I was really going to have to take it to the next level in order to achieve my lofty goal of receiving a full scholarship to a Division I College Football Program. Since my weight lifting habits were year round, I was back in the gym lifting weights and adding bulk to my 185-lb frame.

Prior to the start of my senior year at CHS, my good friend, Dan Rupert, and I decided to take a trip up to the University of Michigan for a training camp that lasted a week. If there ever was a good word of advice for college football prospects, this is it, so listen up! I remember one of the college coaches from Michigan coming to our school for a visit. He said they were having a special camp for college recruits which he highly recommended attending. The cost for the week would be around $300, but if they were interested enough in my football talent, it was possible that I could be offered a full scholarship at the camp. The recruiter made the training camp sound like a special "invite" event, where I would be working exclusively with the linebacker coach. However, when we got to the University, there were over 300 college recruits in attendance. It was a deceiving way to get as many college recruits to the University of Michigan for the training camp and to make as much money as possible.

There was one player who stood out at the camp, and by his size and speed you could tell that he was going to be something special. His name was Curtis Enis, and he probably weighed about 225 lbs at the time. He was getting clocked in the 40-yard dash in the low 4.4's and you could tell the Michigan coaches were drooling about him possibly playing for the Wolverines. Unfortunately for Michigan, Curtis had another team in mind. He ended up signing his letter of intent to play for the Penn State Nittany Lions. After a successful college career as a running back, he was drafted in the first round of the NFL draft by the Chicago Bears.

I am not going to say college-training camps for college recruits are not beneficial, because they are good places to go to learn skills to take with you into your college career. What I would not recommend is running the 40-yard dash at any of these camps unless you plan on getting a stellar time that you can brag about to your friends. I made the mistake of running the 40-yard dash and was clocked at an unusually slow time of 5.02 seconds, when I had run high 4.8 to 4.9's in the past. Little did I know that this information would be shared with college coaches around the country. Guess what the first thing a lot of coaches asked me? That's right; they would say, "I heard you ran a 5.02 at the University of Michigan Training Camp".

A SENIOR SEASON OF UPS AND DOWNS

The emphasis of my training for the senior football season was primarily focused on gaining as much weight as possible, getting stronger and running faster, simple strategies to take it up a level on the football field. I saw myself inflate from 185 lbs to about 220 lbs in a single year. The credit for this weight gain can be attributed to hard work in the weight room but especially to all those home cooked meals by mom, high grocery bills and a strong growth spurt during the summer of '93.

Entering into the '93 season, I was selected as preseason All-Pioneer Conference at the middle linebacker position and was listed in multiple college football recruiting magazines as an upcoming player to scout. I was already receiving recruiting letters in the mail and started to make plans to visit colleges I was interested in before the season had even begun. It was an exciting time of seeing everything unfold around me as years of hard work were paying off.

The start of doubles during the mid-summer heat of August proved to display an unexpected twist to the beginning of my senior season. During one of the drills during doubles, I pulled my groin and was limited during double sessions. Even though I was legitimately injured, it is hard for other players to be toiling under the hot summer heat and not feel a little resentment towards the player who does not have to go full speed. This resulted in losing some credibility with the players, and when it was time to select team captains, the most heavily recruited college player on the team was left out.

Respect is something on the football field that will never be given to you. It is something that must be earned through sacrificing it all and giving 100% on every play. When it is all on the line and someone either has to score or defend the end zone, the person willing to go above and beyond will earn not only the respect of his teammates but also his opponents. Although I was disappointed about not being selected as a captain, I vowed to spend the entire season earning the respect of my teammates by my unselfish play on the field.

The 1993 Cloverleaf football team had high expectations due to the success experienced in the prior season. A considerable amount of starters returned on both sides, and even a highly touted running back transferred from one of our rival schools. The season started out with three impressive non-conference victories. The defense allowed only one touchdown in the three wins. We were picking up momentum, and everyone immediately started saying that this was the year we would go to the state playoffs.

Just as quickly as the season started out red hot, our luck suddenly flew south for three weeks as we lost three games in a row. The first two losses were by a total of two points and the third loss was an old-fashioned beating by the Midpark Meteors as they ran over and through us to win 35-14. It was gut check time and even though we had lost three games in a row, we were still 3-3. It was time for the seniors to take charge and that is just what we did as we demolished the Brecksville Bees the following week by a score of 27-3.

I wish I could say that that we won the last three games of the season and the Cloverleaf Colts went to the state playoffs for the first time in school history, but it was not meant to be. We did win two of the last three games and finished a respectable 6-4 for a football program that was consistently below .500 before the '92 season. The funny thing was that if we went 7-3, there was a good chance we would have had enough points to make school history. We were one game short just like the prior year, but on a bright note, the Berea Braves who crushed our playoff dreams the year before with the tomahawk chop were defeated for the first time in our school's history by a score of 27-20.

The season came to an end but the memories of high school football still live on and are replayed in my mind. That year I ended the season with over 150 tackles and averaged over 15 per game. My stats were good enough to earn me First Team All-Pioneer Conference and First Team All-District. College scouts from schools like Purdue, Syracuse, Kentucky and many more came to our games to see a high school player living out his dream on 120 yards of marked and painted grass. I left it all on the field that season and when it was all said and done, I earned back the respect of my teammates. That was more important to me than winning games or going to the playoffs, because wins and losses are forgotten but relationships with good friends can last a lifetime.

There are two things about my senior year that I will always cherish. The first was my last home game at Cloverleaf stadium. As we walked down the hill to the end zone for the last time, I remember standing under the goal post and looking up at the American Flag as the national anthem was being played. I could smell the popcorn in the stands and the faint smell of cigar smoke in the air. It was a beautiful night under those Friday night football lights, and there was a gentle, cool breeze. Everything felt right in the world, and I realized at that moment how lucky I was to live in the United States of America and to be able to play the best sport in the world. A tear ran down my cheek at that moment, and it was as if I knew that football would never be this much fun again. We were just a bunch of kids playing football on a Friday night among all our family and friends. There were no hidden agendas and no politics - just some good old-fashioned football.

The second memory that I hold close to my heart is the last game of the season against the Medina Bees. It was getting close to the end of the game, and my head coach decided to put my younger brother in the game to play linebacker beside me. The Viera brothers were out on the field together, in the midst of battle. There was something special and unforgettable about sharing the last moments of my high school football career with my brother. He had always been a great supporter, and now we have this memory of playing together that will last us a lifetime.

RECRUITING CALLS, LETTERS AND VISITS

Before student athletes can play at the college level, they are required to register with the NCAA Initial-Eligibility Clearinghouse. This organization partners with the NCAA to determine whether a student athlete is eligible for collegiate athletic participation during their first year. Eligibility is determined by review of high school transcripts, ACT or SAT scores, and any applicable information regarding amateurism participation. This is a crucial step during the recruiting process because if your eligibility is not cleared, you will not be permitted to play college sports your first year. This inevitably makes it more difficult to be recruited because you would be labeled "ineligible."

I highly encourage student athletes to visit the NCAA online for additional information regarding preparation for "The College-Bound Student-Athlete," "Transfer Guide," and "A Career in Professional Athletics." Being informed and educated about your upcoming decisions will allow for a smooth transition. These different guides list questions that should be asked regarding choosing the right college, financial aid, and prospective agents, if you are blessed enough to play at the professional level.

The college recruiting process is something that I made the most of and fully enjoyed my senior year. I have heard stories of parents pressuring their children to do all they can to get a full scholarship, and in the process, they lost the thrill of the chase. I remember when I received my first college-recruiting letter in the mail during the end of my junior year and got a little excited.

There are many different facets of the recruiting process. There are informal letters and formal letters delivered in the mail from college universities and college football recruiters. The ones to get a little excited about are the letters that are hand written by the coaches themselves. There are visits by the recruiting coaches to the school where the coach is not permitted to talk to you before a certain time in the recruiting season, due to the NCAA recruiting rules and regulations. That is when you simply have a coach excuse you from class so you can walk down the hall in front of the college coach and they can see if you are a good size for the position they are interested in having you play.

I can remember when one of the coaches from the University of Kentucky came to the school but was not allowed to talk to me. I might have gotten an inside tip from my head coach of the visit, so I decided to wear my rattlesnake cowboy boots to school. This not only gave the perception that I was taller than I actually was, but if the recruiter enjoyed country music, he probably thought I had a little style. Believe it or not, the recruiter measured me with my boots on to see how tall I was, compared to the measurements he was given. With an extra two inches of elevation I was pushing an impressive 6'3.

After the season was complete, there were around 28 Division I and Division I AA College football programs recruiting me. Senior linebackers in high school that were 6'1 and 220 lbs were a valuable commodity to college football programs. I was fortunate enough to have received letters from multiple schools that were displaying interest in my abilities and even got calls from coaches on a weekly basis right up to the national signing day of February 2, 1994.

As the year was coming to a close, the recruiting process really started to heat up. You can get all the letters in the world from college coaches and your phone can be ringing off the hook, but unless you get invited to a recruiting trip by the college you are considering, it does not mean anything. At the time, NCAA rules allowed a recruit to visit up to three schools on recruiting trips where the college paid for the recruit's expenses. Currently, a recruit can take up to five official visits.

Prior to the start of taking my college football recruiting trips, I had the fortunate decision of narrowing down my choices to three schools. I always knew that I wanted to explore all my options, and I took full advantage of the situation. Out of the 28 schools, the three that I chose to visit were Villanova University, Ohio University and the University of Kentucky.

The three schools that I decided to visit all offered excellent college educations and were in three separate football conferences. Villanova University was a Division I AA school located just outside Philadelphia, PA. It was formerly in the Yankee Conference, now known as the Atlantic 10 Conference. The schools Villanova played were predominantly in the northeast. This was my first official recruiting visit.

I remember the excitement of getting to visit Villanova University and seeing the college campus, as well as the athletic facilities, including the football stadium. As my parents and I made the eight-hour drive from Cleveland to VU, we discussed how far I had come and the opportunities that a full scholarship would offer. The idea of going to a college on a full scholarship potentially worth over $100,000 dollars to play a sport that I loved seemed almost too good to be true.

Even though being invited on an official recruiting visit to a University is a nice gesture, it unfortunately does not mean a thing unless the head coach offers you a verbal full scholarship prior to the official signing date on February 2nd. This is important to know for young college recruits because it factors into the schools that you choose to visit. You have to ask yourself, "Has this college been serious in the recruiting process with me, and is there a good chance they are going to offer me a full scholarship?" If the answer is "no," consider the other schools on the table. The last thing you want to do is waste a recruiting trip just to tour a college that you like.

As I went on my first visit, I was paired with one of the starting offensive lineman for the Villanova Wildcats, who also happened to be Spanish. He was assigned to take me around the campus and show me a good time. Something important to note is that as you go on your visits, it is comparable to having your first date with a very attractive woman that you really like. If the woman feels the same way about you, both sides are going to try their best to be polite and considerate. Neither person is going to show any of their flaws, and cautious, carefully selected words are used so as not to offend or scare away the person each one is trying to impress. In other words, you try to paint the prettiest picture imaginable for the other person to take in and enjoy. A college recruiting trip has all these qualities and characteristics. The difference is that instead of being paired with an attractive female, there is a college football player telling you why this is the college for you. They want you to enjoy the experience as much as possible so when they say those magic words, "We want you to play for us, and we are offering you a full scholarship", you will jump at the opportunity.

Based on NCAA recruiting rules and regulations at the time I was being recruited, players were each given $40 to spend on their recruit for the weekend. After touring the college and meeting with the coaches on the first day, that night we went out to a club to explore the nightlife. Little did they know that I did not drink, especially since the legal drinking age is 21 and I was only 17 years old. Now I know that some of you are thinking, "Why in the world didn't you drink, especially when they were paying for it?" For me, the answer is quite simple. I think one of the biggest misconceptions about college and life in general is that you can only have a good time if you are drinking alcohol. Everyone has the freedom to make decisions for themselves. The reason that I did not drink was because I could not think how it would make me a better football player. Why would I invest so much time and energy toward advancing and enhancing my linebacker abilities and then do something that would hinder my performance and ultimately my potential? It just did not make sense.

Before I knew it, the trip to VU came to a close, and the next thing I knew I was sitting in the head coach's office with the assistant head coach. Just as I had imagined in my dreams, I heard the head coach say those magic words that so many college football recruits are waiting to hear before signing day. The head coach said I had the talent to play linebacker at VU, and they were willing to offer me a full scholarship, if I would give them a verbal commitment. This is where you walk a real fine line of making sure that the recruiting trips you have set up are going to be offering the same results. There is a small window of opportunity to play college football on a full scholarship, and you have to make sure the decisions you make are the right ones before that window closes on February 2nd.

That day I had to decline for the moment their scholarship offer until I took my visits to Ohio University and the University of Kentucky. It was a big risk to take, especially because they were recruiting other linebackers, who were also talented and might make early verbal commitments. I had a good feeling that the other two schools would also offer scholarships due to my conversations with the coaches recruiting me, but a feeling is not equal to a guarantee.

The next visit was to Ohio University, a Division I School that plays in the Mid-American Football Conference commonly referred to as the MAC. This school also offered an excellent education and had great facilities, but unlike VU, they played big name schools like Syracuse, Purdue and Michigan in their non-conference games. This offered the opportunity to be seen on national television, which is always something nice for family members to watch on a Saturday afternoon. They were also only a four-hour drive from Cleveland, while it was an eight-hour drive to VU.

The outcome of the trip was the same with a scholarship offer from the head coach. However, I had to decline for the moment, awaiting my final visit to the University of Kentucky. While VU waited patiently to hear from me after my visit to UK, Ohio University was not as patient, and before my last visit, called to say another linebacker they were interested in had committed. They no longer needed to fill a linebacker position. Just like that, they were marked off my list of potential places to go. I was left with one last college to visit and if my gut feeling of being offered another scholarship did not pan out, I would have VU on the back burner. Of course, VU was not a guarantee because they could also end up filling their linebacker need like Ohio University. You can see how this whole recruiting process can bring stress and drama into your life. It is like living in a college recruiting soap opera.

CATCHING WILDCAT FEVER

The last visit finally came, and it was definitely the most anticipated recruiting trip. I must admit that I never knew that the University of Kentucky had a football team prior to their recruiting me, but they seemed to have everything I was looking for in a college. The thing that probably stuck out the most was the college recruiter by the name of Coach Ray Dorr. From day one of the recruiting process, Coach Dorr could not have done a better job of getting me to think about the possibility of playing football at UK. It seemed like I was getting a letter from UK just about every week in the mail and once the recruiters had the green light to call players at their home, I talked to Coach Dorr on several different occasions. He upheld such a courteous and professional relationship; you would want him to remain your friend even if UK was not a good fit.

An opportunity to play at UK was something that I had been hoping would come true ever since the recruiting process first started. They are in arguably one of the toughest football conferences in the country. The Southeastern Conference or SEC has all the big name schools that are broadcast nationally on television. Schools like Tennessee, Auburn, Alabama, Florida, LSU and Georgia had top rate caliber players destined for the NFL like Peyton Manning, Stephen Davis, Shaun Alexander, Danny Wuerffel, Jerome Kearse, Kevin Faulk and Hines Ward. The opportunity to play against these players was something that I was not going to pass up if given the opportunity. You only get one go around to play college football, and I wanted it to be with the best this country had to offer!

To sweeten the pot even more, UK went to the Peach Bowl in 2003 and nearly defeated the Clemson Tigers in a nail-biter 13-14. The opportunity to be able to play in bowl games on national television was a nice incentive. In addition, the fact that UK's senior middle linebacker, Marty Moore, was drafted by the New England Patriots in the 1994 NFL Draft meant that it could possibly offer the opportunity to play at the next level after college. Even though he was the last pick in the draft which is called "Mr. Irrelevant" and a parade was thrown for him at Disney World for this honor, he was still drafted just like all the players before him and now wears a Super Bowl ring.

As you can probably tell by now, choosing Kentucky was a slam-dunk decision. During my recruiting trip, it was easy to tell that their athletic facilities were by far the best in the country. They did not have the biggest stadium, which was approximately 60,000 capacity at the time (compared to stadiums like Tennessee and Michigan that are over 100,000 in capacity). Nevertheless, if you combine their stadium with the indoor facility that is 132,000 square feet and the Nutter Center that is over 48,000 square feet in size (consisting of a 20,000 square feet weight room, indoor glass racquetball courts and an incredible locker room with a sauna, jacuzzi and a powerade dispenser), it was an unbeatable combination. It was said that the football team spent over $100,000 in supplements a year for the football players. This was not difficult to believe after seeing the supply room that had shelves bulging with protein powder, creatine, vitamins, protein bars and every imaginable protein shake or drink on the market. The fact that they had a players lounge with a pool table and a big screen television made this facility feel more like a vacation getaway.

The recruiting trip to UK could not have gone better. The way to an athlete's heart is through his stomach and the steak and crab legs that were served during the recruiting trip made UK hard to forget. It was easy to be impressed with the facilities but more importantly, their head coach, Bill Curry, was someone who took pride in having his players make the most of their college education. Coach Curry played center in the NFL with the Baltimore Colts and Green Bay Packers with quarterback legends, Johnny Unitas and Bart Star. He saw what could happen to a player's career in a single play and knew the true value of a good college education. This is the type of coach that you want to play for in college.

The weekend recruiting trip encompassed all the college recruits for the same weekend instead of splitting up the weekends. This meant that if you were offered a scholarship and you felt like this was the place for you, there was not much time to waste in making a decision, especially since the trip was in January, and signing day was right around the corner, on February 2nd. When it was my turn to talk to Coach Curry after the weekend festivities, it felt as if I answered his question almost before he could ask it. He wanted me to play middle linebacker at the University of Kentucky and was offering me a full scholarship. As I committed right then and there, it was as if an incredible weight had been lifted off of my shoulders. My college was finally chosen after the anticipated recruiting process. It was like hitting the lottery for over $100,000 dollars, because the next four to five years would not cost a single cent. Little did I know what it would do to my body physically.

As I signed my letter of intent on February 2, 1993, the dream of a young child had been fulfilled. Now it was time to set my sights even higher. The prospect of studying medicine to become a doctor and the possibility of playing in the NFL danced in my head. The future was slowly unfolding before my eyes but time would only tell what would transpire. Besides, I still had to make it past my first semester at UK.

CHAPTER THREE

FIRST SEMESTER AT COLLEGE

Let your light so shine before men, that they may see your good works and glorify your father in heaven.
- MATTHEW 5:16

You are of God, little children and have overcome them, because He who is in you is greater than he who is in the world.
- 1 JOHN 4:4

To be yourself in a world that is constantly trying to make you something else is the greatest accomplishment.
- RALPH WALDO EMERSON

WALKING OH HIGHER GROUND AND AWAKENING THE SPIRIT WITHIN

*T*he summer of 1993 was ending and it was almost time to report to UK for a series of freshman football practices before double practices started for the upcoming college season. All summer I had lifted weights and performed the cardiovascular exercises given to me by the UK strength coach in the mail. I wanted to be in the best shape possible and start my freshman year on a good note weighing a solid 220 lbs. The middle linebacker position was vacant due to Marty Moore's being a senior. If I had anything to do with it, I was going to learn the defensive playbook and compete for the starting position.

There are seldom times in a person's life when he truly feels the power of freedom. Two such times I can remember in my life were when I first learned to drive and got the opportunity to drive myself to work at Hawkins' Supermarket to work in the produce department. I was 16 years old and I can still hear the country music that was turned up a little too loud. The cool breeze was blowing on my arm that was hanging out the window and the feel of control with a dash of power overwhelmed me as I tightly gripped that steering wheel with my one hand and drove unsupervised for the first time.

The second time that freedom really took on a completely different meaning was when my parents drove me to UK to drop me off for my freshman year. I can remember the anticipation and excitement of thinking about the future experiences I would encounter as a student athlete at UK. As we arrived at the University, everything I needed from the van was placed into my dorm room. After spending some time with my parents and introducing them to my new roommate, we said our "goodbyes," and they drove back to Medina, OH. There I was, lying on my bed in the dorm room, 18 years old and on my own for the first time. I think the feeling I felt was not necessarily freedom from my parents, because we have always had a good relationship. It was more a freedom of responsibility.

In a sudden instant, I was transformed from being a teen to a responsible adult - a student athlete that had to be accountable for his actions and not willing to settle for mediocrity. I knew I must be brave enough to say "no" to something that was not right. I must be strong enough to be a leader, instead of following the pack. Once you get to college, you have to be prepared to face trials and tribulations of all sorts.

You have to be ready to make difficult decisions in the face of adversity. That is unfortunately the life and responsibility of a student athlete. You have more people than you know watching your every move and waiting to say, "He's just another typical student athlete who is a poor role model." The challenge is to prove them wrong and differentiate yourself from the others. The question is, "Are you up for the challenge and are you willing to stand up for what you believe in?"

ROOMMATE GRANDE

Regardless of what college you decide to attend, there is one thing that is as certain as the sun rising in the morning and setting at dusk. That one universal thing is that you are going to have countless stories that will last a lifetime about your college roommates. The roommate process for freshman college athletes is always interesting because you don't really have a choice of whom you are going to be paired with for a minimum of a semester. During the recruiting trip, you meet recruits for the first time, and before you know it, you start the first semester at college, living with someone you hardly know.

I will never forget walking into my dorm room for the first time. My college football roommate was an offensive lineman that stood 6'7 and weighed 265 lbs. He extended his long arm to shake my hand and I knew things were about to get interesting. Let me tell you that dorm rooms are not as spacious as one might think and if you toss in an offensive lineman that is 6'7 with size 18 shoes, your world tends to feel a little smaller. Now I'm not going to say that we did not have anything in common because we both played football, but besides that, we were total opposites. My roommate was raised on a pig farm in Midwestern Ohio and graduated from a high school in a small town with a senior graduating class of about 30 students. Needless to say, he was not the cleanest person in the world and had a strong tendency to drink on the weekends with so many of the other freshman.

So how do you maintain the lifestyle that you are accustomed to living while sharing a dorm room with someone who is totally opposite? The answer to that question is quite simple. You set your own standards and hope that some of your positive traits rub off on your roommate. The one thing you cannot be afraid of is the feeling of rejection from players if you are not willing to partake in extracurricular activities like drinking or smoking. The fact is that if they are your friends, they will respect you for your personal decision. Besides, deep down inside, they are probably envious because you have made a decision that many college athletes are not able to make regarding alcohol and smoking.

Now there is always the chance that your good example produces little change in your roommate by the end of the semester. If this happens, don't get discouraged, because you always have the option of swapping roommates with another football player as I did. You may have to grin and bear your gloomy predicament for a semester, but when that semester is over, it's time to wheel-and-deal to find a more suitable roommate. Sometimes the trick can be finding someone who actually wants to live with your roommate. Luckily for myself, that was not hard due to the number of drinking buddies he had in the dorm.

During my first semester at UK, the weekend would roll around, and we would each be given $40 for meal money. An alarming amount of the freshman players would head straight to the liquor store and buy 24 packs of beer and hard liquor like Jim Bean, vodka, or whiskey. I'm not quite sure how much they actually ate during those weekends, with all the drinking that was going on in the dorm. Do you know what I did with my $40 dollars each weekend? I know some of you might laugh, but I walked to the nearest Kroger grocery store and actually used my money for what it was intended for. I bought food. I can still remember sitting in my dorm room during those freshman weekends. While my roommate and other freshman players were drinking alcohol, I would be eating a mango and drinking Gatorade.

Although a full scholarship can be good for four to five years, the one thing coaches fail to mention during recruitment is that it is contingent on a year-to-year basis. That means that the head coach has to make the annual decision of whether your scholarship will be renewed. I worked extremely hard to get my full scholarship to UK. I was not about to let anything get in the way of playing college football, and more importantly, getting a quality college education. If that meant that I had to walk on the road less traveled by many college athletes, then that was exactly what I intended to do.

FIRST SEMESTER AT COLLEGE

PUTTING ON THE RED SHIRT

To this day I truly believe football teaches you more about life than any other sport. It is a game of teamwork, heart and even self sacrifice. The last of those three things is what I experienced most my first season at UK. It was not long after the excitement of being away at college that the time came to get down to business. Let's face it: College football is a business. There is a reason you get to attend college for free. The fans long to see the players on the field, and you are the reason they line up to get autographs. Revenue from ticket sales, advertisements on television and money given to colleges for bowl game appearances far exceed a couple of million dollars during the course of a season. The great football machine is a money-making, revenue-generating "cash cow" for every University.

After checking into the dorm, it was not long before we had our first football meeting with all the freshman players and the coaches. We were given our playbooks to get familiar with and a schedule to follow for double practices. Freshman players report earlier than veteran players so they can get a jump start on understanding how the offense or defense works, depending upon what position you play. For myself, it was a defensive playbook that seemed thicker than a giant-sized telephone book. Due to the secrecy of material in the playbooks, we were basically instructed to guard the books with our lives. The last thing you want to do as a freshman is lose your playbook and have it get into the wrong hands before the start of the season.

My first college football practice is still fresh in my mind. There were definitely butterflies in my stomach that day as I performed the drills we were instructed to do. Perhaps this was caused by all the media that was at practice, taking pictures of our every move. All the attention made me feel like a robot as I did a bag drill or ran to catch a pass. Needless to say, my performance at the first practice did not exactly turn any heads - not a good start for someone who wanted to compete for the starting middle linebacker position at a college football program in the SEC.

After getting in some quality practices for the first few days of freshman doubles, it was time for the big boys to start practicing with us. It's hard to forget seeing the upper classmen players for the first time. If you have ever seen the movie, "Pumping Iron," with Arnold

Swartzenegger, it was very similar to when Lou Ferrigno saw Arnold in person for the first time. He turned to his father and said, "Boy, Dad, he's big!" That is about the reaction I had when I first started seeing the players walking into the locker room. I was an eighteen year old teenager, getting ready to bang pads with young men in their early twenties.

As double practices got into full swing in the humid summer heat of the Bluegrass state, there was little time to think about anything except playing football. The morning began with breakfast about 7 a.m., morning position meetings, and the morning practice, which lasted about two hours. Lifting was required four times a week to keep up your strength, usually after the first or second practice. After taking a shower and drinking plenty of fluids to rehydrate yourself, it was off to lunch. If you were a fast eater, you could sneak back to your dorm room to get in a 45 minute power nap before heading back to the Nutter Center for afternoon team and position meetings. Afternoon practice lasted roughly two hours, and then it was time for dinner at the mess hall. The evening was reserved for position meetings, to review practice and critique the players so they could improve. After about 9 p.m., you had the rest of the day to yourself before doing it all over again the following day.

It did not take too many double practices before I started getting anxious for college classes to start. My body was exhausted, and by the looks of my location on the depth chart for middle linebacker, it was looking more and more every day like I was going to be redshirted. It did not help that my position coach was not exactly the kind of person you would call a player's coach. He definitely was not one to encourage you with kind words. He seemed to like the tough guy image and would try to break you down at every opportunity. I can remember very few times that he ever even smiled.

Now for those of you who do not know what being redshirted means, I will elaborate for you. Once a college football player enrolls in a University, he has five years to play four years of football. This is made possible because coaches can decide whether they want to play a freshman his first year or redshirt him. The second option would allow the player to get stronger and faster for the following season without losing a year of eligibility, hence, having five years to play four. Once that window is closed, the only way someone can possibly get an additional year is by qualifying for a medical redshirt. This can happen when a player has a season-ending injury that results in his missing the greater portion of the season. The reason it is called "redshirting" is because the player participates in every practice as a member of the scout team, wearing a red shirt. He continues to do the lifting program and goes to all the meetings; however, when it is time for a game, the true freshman usually does not get to dress and will probably be watching the game from the stands.

This sounds like a raw deal but you really have to step back and look at the bigger picture. For any freshman player who is redshirted, it is never easy to sit back and watch your team play its opponents on Saturday afternoons. The reason I know this is because I ended up getting redshirted my freshman year along with a majority of our freshman class. The players in our recruiting class had signed their letters of intent a couple of months after UK's appearance in the Peach Bowl against the Clemson Tigers. The 1994 University of Kentucky freshman recruiting class ranked 13th in the country. The majority of our freshman class was redshirted. These were very talented athletes being recruited by top-notch colleges all over the country before signing to play at UK. Being redshirted did not mean that we lacked the talent to play at the SEC level; it just meant we needed a little more time to develop physically and mentally as players.

If you have been recently redshirted, let me be the first one to congratulate you on this accomplishment. That might seem like a strange thing to pat someone on the back for achieving but let me explain. The first and most important benefit you have just gained is another year of college at no monetary cost to you. Your education is the one college experience that will last you a lifetime. Once you obtain your bachelor's degree, no one can take it away from you. This extra year can be used to pursue a double major or even start working on your master's degree. In addition, you will have more time to focus on your studies and build a solid academic base for your G.P.A. By the way, you also just earned free weekends to yourself with no football responsibilities when the team is playing away.

Now some of you are saying to yourselves, "Man, I came here to play football and not sit on the bench." You might not be fully interested in the educational aspect of the college experience because your master plan consists of playing in the NFL and being set for life. Now there is nothing wrong with making the prospect of playing in the NFL a goal for your life. I think everyone should shoot for the stars and try to outlive their dreams. All I am saying is that in life you should always have a Plan B just in case the unthinkable happens. If you are drafted in the NFL, how long do you think it will last? I can assure you it will not be a lifetime like a college education. That is why I think it is wise to make that plan B a college degree.

The opportunity to be redshirted gives you another year to grow physically and mentally. In most cases, it is the best thing that can happen to you, long-term. I know countless players who were not redshirted their first year of college and regret having a season being wasted on special teams and occasionally getting to play their position when the score was out of reach. The redshirt will allow you to get a better understanding of the offensive or defensive systems that are used, and your chance of being a true student of the game will greatly increase. Lastly, just like Rocky, you will get the "Eye of the Tiger" for the upcoming season. Hopefully you already have it but I am talking about an enhanced eagerness to play the game at a level that you could never have imagined.

The one thing that a redshirt certainly does not exclude you from is freshman hazing. Depending on where you go to college this process can vary in intensity and duration. Some upperclassmen have all the freshmen shave their heads. Others might take turns giving all the freshmen wedgies. My freshman class had to memorize the UK fight song and sing it in front of the upperclassmen in the dorm on a selected night. I know you're thinking that is a simple test; however, you had to be wearing nothing but your boxers and drink a dixie cup full of a special concoction created by the seniors. The ingredients were not openly discussed with the freshman but I remember it being hot and spicy. There is a good possibility that a large amount of hot sauce was used. There was a rumor that some snuff might have been one of the mixed ingredients but that was just speculation. As we sang the fight song in selected groups that night after drinking the strange brew, I vividly remember a cornerback in my group sweating profusely as he was singing the fight song and clapping his hands. It must have been some good hot sauce they used.

OVERLOOKED BENEFITS OF A BACHELOR'S DEGREE

There are many benefits that are associated with a bachelor's degree besides the fact that you will be more marketable in the workplace. According to the National Center for Education Statistics (NCES),

> In 2001, the better educated a person was, the more likely that person was to report being in "excellent" or "very good" health. Among adults age 25 and over, 78 percent of those with bachelor's degree or higher reported being in excellent or very good health, compared with 66 percent of those with some education beyond high school, 56 percent of high school completers, and 39 percent of those with less than a high school education.

In addition, to having a better chance of being in excellent health, a bachelor's degree can also increase your chances of making it to the NFL. According to the National Football League Players Association (NFLPA),

> Education is crucial for success to become an NFL player or a success at any career. Completing a college degree will not only prepare players for life after football, but it also seems to pay off during a player's career. Players with degrees earn 20 to 30% more than players who don't have degrees. They also have a career that lasts about 50% longer. While there is not one answer for why players with degrees have strong careers, one theory is that players who show the intelligence, concentration, and mental discipline to complete a degree show these qualities on the field more. Doing well in school from an early age also helps players develop concentration they will need to memorize plays and avoid eligibility problems in high school and college.

If the NFLPA is saying that about education and they work for the players, it shows the real importance of getting a bachelor's degree in college. Now before you get all excited about what team you are going to be playing for in the NFL, let me run some alarming statistics by you. According to the NFLPA, "statistically of the 100,000 high school seniors who play football every year, only 215 will ever make an NFL roster." That comes out to a whopping 0.2% chance of making it to the NFL! The NFLPA also says, "Even of the 9,000 players that make it to the college level only 310 are invited to the NFL scouting combine, the pool from which teams make their draft picks." That leaves you with a 3% chance of playing on Sundays in the fall.

There seems to be a general misunderstanding among college football players that if you make it to the NFL, you are automatically going to be a millionaire. According to the NFLPA, "In 2000, the minimum salary for rookies was $193,000. While the highest paid players in the league can make $7-$8 million per year, most players make much less than that." In 2005, the league minimum salary was raised to $230,000. Of course, your NFL salary comes with benefits like dental, medical, disability, pre-season pay, severance pay and pension coverage. The problem is that with an average NFL career lasting only three and a half seasons, you really need to be a savvy investor to make your NFL earnings last a lifetime.

Let's say you were to get drafted, are better than the average NFL rookie, and pull in $300,000 a year for 4 years. That probably sounds pretty good to a lot of you reading this right now. You may be thinking, "Man, what I could do with $1.2 million dollars!" Before you start spending your money, we have to give Uncle Sam a piece of the pie. It is really more like a chunk of the pie when you consider that you'll be paying at least 33% in federal taxes, 5-6% in state taxes, 6.2% in Social Security taxes up to the first $90,000, 1.45% for Medicare taxes and most likely, fees associated with the NFLPA. So what does that roughly leave you with? Suddenly your $300,000 a year salary has turned into approximately $165,000 a year!

When you factor in the fact that professional players buy sports cars or expensive SUV's exceeding $50,000 and that a nice houses can be between $200,000 to $300,000, there is not a great deal of money left. That $165,000 a year for four years is $660,000. After you subtract the $50,000 for the car and approximately $250,000 for a house, you have $360,000 left. When you consider that the remaining money has to last you a lifetime due to not committing yourself to getting a bachelor's degree, things look pretty bleak. Let's assume you started in the NFL at age 22 and that your career will end at age 26. If we predict that you may live to the age of 70 and divide the remaining $360,000 by 44 years, you have a minuscule $8,182 a year to work with, considering no supplemental income.

Now consider what you could have earned if you got a bachelor's degree in a major like Accounting or Finance. You can easily earn $45,000 to $55,000 a year. If we multiply $50,000 by 44 years you will earn $2.2 million dollars over your lifetime after your career in the NFL. That is not even taking into account the annual cost-of-living raises or a 401K savings plan that can be earning interest on your pre-tax dollars. It definitely pays to study hard and earn that degree.

STATE-OF-THE-ART FOOTBALL GEAR

Doubles during my freshman year were a whirlwind of excitement. Besides all of the grunt work during practices as a scout member of the defense, there were exciting things taking place. Due to UK's Nike football contract, each year every team member received a new pair of Nike's latest and greatest athletic shoes. Those sweet kicks could not even be found at your local shoe store. The reason athletic shoe companies love to supply Division I football programs with free football gear is because when you are playing on ABC or ESPN it is an excellent way for them to advertise their name. Athletic shoe companies have been known to pay the universities of the bigger college football programs more than a million dollars to be able to supply free football gear to the players. Every marketing manager knows that nothing says "Buy Me" to a young kid more than watching a football player catch a pass with his Nike gloves on national television and waltz 50 yards for a touchdown sporting his Nike cleats. Every player on our team received four pairs of shoes a year. We received a trendy Nike athletic pair to wear to college classes on campus, a pair of Nike astro turf shoes, a pair of Nike practice cleats and a pair of Nike cleats for games.

The equipment room at UK was unlike anything I had ever seen. It would give Foot Locker or even Sports Authority a good run for its money. Regardless of what type of athletic accessory you were interested in to compliment your standard football equipment, they had just what you wanted. Most everyone who watches football on Saturday or Sunday knows that standard football equipment consists of the helmet, shoulder pads, hip pads, knee pads, thigh pads and a tail bone pad. Of course, if you are watching the NFL, some players, like the receivers, just wear the shoulder pads and helmet.

Let's say you were in UK's equipment room and you wanted a visor for your helmet. Not a problem. Consider it a done deal. Maybe you're looking for receiving gloves or lineman gloves. All you had to do was pick the style you wanted. I would compare my experience in UK's equipment room to a sugar-craving child in a candy store. Everything looked so good you wanted to try one of everything. The options I chose to go with my standard equipment were elbow pads, linemen gloves, additional knee pads and a neck brace.

There is one thing I know for certain about football, and that is, that danger is always present on the field. You have to protect yourself, and that is just what I tried to do. On the first day of full contact during freshman practice, my linebacker coach called me "Pad Man" when he saw me in pads. The mistake I made that day was wearing the elbow and knee pads instead of getting the sleeves. Not only do the sleeves look cooler but they are less bulky, lighter and a tighter fit. Needless to say, after the first day of full contact practice, I was sporting the new elbow and knee sleeves. Rest assured that "Pad Man" is not the type of nickname you want during your collegiate football career. That is right up there with being called "Cotton" for being soft. Luckily for me, the nickname did not last more than a couple of days.

AUTOGRAPHS AND MORE AUTOGRAPHS

During the end of double practices, right before the start of college classes, UK held its Annual Football Fan Day. It was located at Commonwealth Stadium field for all the fans to meet and greet the players. The players wore their home field game jersey, pants and new Nike shoes. I remember some players did not want to wear their new shoes because they were afraid they would get grass stains on their sweet kicks. The coaches did not give them an option, so they had to suck it up and take their chances with the grass.

As a freshman who had not even played a single down for UK, I was not expecting to sign any autographs for the fans. In college football I figured that kind of stuff was reserved for the quarterbacks, running backs and receivers who score all the touchdowns. Besides, a little over three months ago I had just graduated from high school and recently moved out of my parent's house. I was not exactly the type of person you would approach for an autograph. Much to my surprise, that day I must have signed over 100 autographs. I signed media guides, UK banners, footballs, baseball caps, posters and notebooks. There were even fans that had their pictures taken with me. I would be lying if I said I did not sneak in a couple of bicep flexes during some of those pictures.

Fan Day at Commonwealth Stadium boasted a strong showing of parents with their children who wanted nothing more than to get everyone's signature on the football team. Some of the fans even knew the freshman players by name, what position they played and where they were from, because they were die hard Wildcat fans. It was a humbling experience signing autographs and getting my picture taken with our fans as if I were some sort of a celebrity. It was also a small taste of what it would be like to live the life of a bright and shining college football star. One thing was for sure that day, it was a rock-solid confirmation that Wildcat fans not only bleed blue, but were and always will be the best fans in the country.

PICKING THE PERFECT MAJOR

It was finally time for college classes to start. The sound of college students on campus was refreshing after being with football players for over two weeks. Students who were rushing for a fraternity or sorority were on campus about a week before classes started, and the campus suddenly stopped feeling like a ghost town, and more like a bustling campus. It also presented an opportunity for football players to partake in the drinking activities during rush week. This was another obstacle for the players to overcome as they prepared for the first game of the season against the Louisville Cardinals.

Doubles felt like it lasted several months, but it had only been a couple of weeks. Prior to the start of the first semester, all the freshman players registered early for their classes. This was crucial, because your classes had to be either between 7 a.m. and 12 p.m. or after dinner, which was around 6 p.m. to 7 p.m. This was due to the block reserved for football meetings and practices in the afternoons. If you registered early, you were pretty much guaranteed to get the classes at the times you wanted before enrollment reached capacity.

Another advantage to having a full scholarship at UK was that when it was time to pick up your books and college supplies at the University book store, everything you needed was neatly placed in a large carryout bag. The person responsible for filling the book orders for the football players would see what classes were being taken and provide every book and study guide applicable for that class. For those of you in college, you know how expensive new course books can cost. Some are easily in the $80 to $100 dollar range for the college core text books. The best part about this whole process was that we would just walk into the bookstore, tell the clerk our names, and they would give us our carryout bag. We signed our name and walked out. If you were taking five to six classes a semester and each course book was over $50 dollars, it would not be uncommon to walk out of the bookstore with $300 to $400 dollars in books.

Each football player was assigned to one of three guidance counselors at the Center for Academic and Tutorial Services known to everyone as CATS. Your guidance counselor would recommend the appropriate classes to take for the semester, based on your selected major. Maybe some of you are saying, "How can I pick a major when I have no idea what I want to do when I graduate college?" That is a valid question; however, before some of you hyperventilate, it is important to know that many college students can go to college for over two years and still be undecided on a major. Even when a major is chosen, many college students change their major several times before they graduate. One of the nice things about college is that it offers you the flexibility to get a feel for what you want to do with your life through all the prerequisite and elective courses that are required. You might start off your first semester taking college courses like Writing 101, Philosophy 101, Sociology 101, Business Analysis 101 and Spanish 101. The beautiful thing is that if you are undecided, these classes will still count towards the credits you need to graduate college.

For myself, there was a reality check my first semester in regard to the major I had originally chosen. Starting out in college, like many youthful and energetic freshman college students across the country, I wanted to be a doctor, and chose Pre-med as my major. How young and foolish I really was back then! My first semester, I took Chemistry 101, which met on Monday, Wednesday and Fridays. When it was time to take the first test, I showed up to class on Friday after a hard week of studying. When I reached the classroom and no one else was there my heart dropped down to my stomach. I knew something was terribly wrong so I called the teacher and found out the test was on Thursday, instead of Friday. Due to the panicked thought of getting a zero on my first college test, I actually got up the courage to meet with the Dean of the Chemistry Department to explain my misunderstanding. After explaining to the Dean what had happened to me, he simply said, "Well, I guess you get a big fat zero." These were not exactly the encouraging words I wanted to hear, but it was an unforgettable lesson, teaching me to pay close attention to details.

The nice thing about college is that you have an allotted window of opportunity to drop a class you have chosen if things start out sour or if you are simply not digging the teacher. As long as the class is dropped in the required period of time, the class is considered a drop and your G.P.A. is not affected. Needless to say, Chemistry 101 was dropped in a heartbeat after receiving a zero on my first test. Instead of taking five classes my first semester, I ended up taking four. This might not seem like a lot, but with football, it was more than enough.

Getting redshirted, missing my first Chemistry test and getting my new mountain bike stolen right in front of my dorm room during my first week on campus was a sure-fire recipe to make my first semester an unforgettable experience. The funny story about my mountain bike is that the bicycle seat was stolen one day and a few days later the bike was stolen. I think I might have actually ridden that new mountain bike a whole two times before it was snatched. I highly encourage any student athlete who brings a bicycle on campus to invest in a quality lock. I unfortunately made the mistake of getting a chain lock, which was most likely cut off when it was stolen.

The following semester I took Chemistry 101 again and made sure I showed up on Thursday to take my first test. Even though I studied as hard as I could, the result of my efforts turned out to be a "C". It was then and there that I made the decision to change my major from Pre-med to Finance. I never looked back after dropping Chemistry 101 for the second consecutive time. It was not necessarily my experience with

Chemistry 101 that persuaded me to change my major, but the fact that I enjoyed business classes more than the science classes. I knew early in the game that I wanted to choose a major that I enjoyed doing wholeheartedly. Ever since I was small, I have been fascinated with the American dollar. I figured a Finance major would allow me to see just how our economy functions on a daily basis and how the dollar can grow over a predetermined period of time in the stock market.

For freshman student athletes looking to choose a college major, I offer these tips that can potentially save you time and heartache. The first thing I would recommend is choosing a major that you can see yourself doing. Many college student athletes have fallen into the trap of choosing the major that is the easiest to complete. I knew many football players who chose Sociology, Communication, Journalism and Education majors, because they knew they would be the majors with the least amount of work. We are at a crucial time in our country where we need more teachers for our school systems, and I salute those who step up to the plate and receive education majors to become teachers. The fact is that these college student athletes were not looking down the road at what they really wanted to be. They simply had their sights set for the NFL, and in the meantime, chose a major that required the least amount of work.

The second trap you can fall into is picking a major based on the amount of money you can earn or the title that comes with a degree. I encourage student athletes and college students in general to look on the internet and do some research on the respective majors that they are considering. It is always nice to know what type of salary range you can expect to receive from your major when you graduate from college. Just keep in mind that the money earned for a particular degree does not always amount to the same level of job satisfaction if you are not enjoying what you are doing. Perhaps you think it would be cool to be called an architect or a marine biologist, but you have no idea what the jobs entail. You need to keep all your options open. There are too many student athletes who go to college for four to five years and then obtain a college degree they cannot use.

Lastly, once you are comfortable with the major you have chosen, I highly encourage student athletes to get familiar with the required classes for completion of your major. After my second trip to the CATS guidance counselor, I had all my classes for the upcoming semester selected prior to my scheduled meeting every semester. You will most likely do a better job of selecting your classes than your guidance counselor. Nobody is going to know what classes you are going to excel at or have difficulty with better than yourself. During college I was very aware of the classes that were required for my major and always tried to pair difficult courses with moderate liberal and free elective courses to balance out the work load with athletics. An example of this would be taking Accounting 201 and Economics 201 with Writing 101, Philosophy 101 and Communications 101. A balanced course load like this will give you the best chance of getting above a 3.0 G.P.A for the semester.

THE LUXURY OF A POWER NAP

Little could prepare me for the rigorous schedule my first semester at college once classes started combined with football responsibilities. One of the many things you have a new found respect for in college is the luxury of a power nap. I can remember countless times in the afternoon where I would head back to the dorm for a little siesta before reporting to the Nutter Facility for football meetings and then practice. Those critical 30-to-45-minute power naps would be just enough to keep me going strong in the afternoon.

The CATS facility had the freshman football players on a strict schedule the first semester. It was necessary to ensure that players were making the most of their time to get ahead on their studies and start out strong. Many players complained about the mandatory two-hour freshman study hall every morning after weight lifting and breakfast that first semester, but I saw it as time well invested. There was plenty of course work to do, and getting a head start on some of it before banging helmets at football practice in the afternoon was all right with me.

A typical day during our first semester consisted of lifting at the Nutter Center at 6 a.m. in the morning, followed by breakfast at the University cafeteria. Everyone who has ever seen or met a football player knows that he likes to eat lots of food. Luckily for us, our meal plan consisted of eating as much and as often as we liked for free - another one of the many perks of being a full scholarship football player. After breakfast, the freshman football players would head back to the Nutter Facility for a mandatory two-hour study hall and then head toward campus to attend one to two college classes before lunch. Typically classes on Monday, Wednesday and Friday were an hour in duration, whereas the classes that met on Tuesday and Thursday were an hour and a half long.

After classes, it would be time for lunch and maybe a quick power nap depending on your class schedule. Are you getting tired yet? I'm getting tired, just thinking about it. After lunch, the players would head over to the Nutter Facility for a brief team meeting, a longer position meeting and then a two-hour football practice. After practice, players would go to the dining hall for dinner and then head to evening class, if applicable. When you think the day is over, that is when you head back to the Nutter Facility to review film of your upcoming opponent. Afterwards, you retire to the dorm for some well deserved sleep before waking up and doing it all over again the next day.

After hearing a schedule like that, you can see that a lot more goes into preparing for a football game than merely getting suited up on a Saturday afternoon. There is a great deal of sacrifice that is required to be a student athlete, and I believe that is one of the reasons that student athletes are admired by their fans. It takes a special person to commit themselves to a sport and put their heart and soul into it day in and day out. Discipline is the cornerstone of success on the football field, and I was certainly learning the ropes my first semester.

CHAPTER FOUR

JUGGLING ACADEMICS, ATHLETICS AND A SOCIAL LIFE

Finding the perfect student athlete balance in college life is an education in itself.
— MIGUEL R. VIERA

He who sows the good seed is the Son of Man.
— MATTHEW 13:37

Success is a state of being. It's knowing where your going and enjoying where you are.
— ANONYMOUS

*H*ow does one begin to even try to find balance for the life of a student athlete? That could very well be a question for the ages. It certainly is not an easy task to accomplish, whether you are a freshman or a fifth-year senior, also known as the infamous super senior. Your time is valuable, and the demands on you are at an all-time high. I was very fortunate to have been a full scholarship football athlete at UK. The cost was supposedly free, but little did I know what "free" meant in the big world of college.

There is an old saying that every economics professor in the country has said ever since students starting lining up to take economics courses. That saying is that "There is no such thing as a free lunch." That could not be truer when it came to playing football at the University of Kentucky. Little did I know that I would be putting in much more than 40 hours a week through classes, coursework and football responsibilities. Needless to say, there were also the physical demands on my body that would push me near the breaking point.

Without a question, you must not only like the sport you are playing in college, but also really love it to be successful. If you are just going through the motions, it is my opinion that you are simply wasting your time. In other words, just taking up space on the team roster and claiming to be something that you are really not. Does any student athlete really want to look back on college ten years from the time he/she graduates and say, "Why did I just go through the motions?" No one ever wants to sit back and reflect on what he or she could have been in college, where they could have gone or what could have possibly been achieved if they had been 100% committed.

That is why being 100% committed from the beginning of college was what I wanted to be all about. The last thing I wanted to do was look back on my college athletic career and think about how I could have done things differently. I wanted to know that there was not an ounce more of energy that I could have put into the game of football or towards my academic pursuit of a bachelor's degree. Fortunately, for myself, I could not get enough of the rigorous and hectic student athlete schedule. I viewed the whole process as not only an induction into manhood but also preparation for the real world, where bills have to be paid on a timely basis, or there are repercussions. It is a world where you and you alone should be solely responsible for providing a roof over your head and putting food on the table. Obtaining over a 3.0 G.P.A my first semester was a solid academic foundation that I could surely build off of in the future.

I am hoping that through this chapter on finding a balance for the student athlete, you can utilize the tools discussed below. They are readily available to help you become successful in your college endeavors. You should enjoy the experiences that come along the way. Not all of them are going to be pleasant and enjoyable, but they will mold you into something that you never possibly thought you could have become in life - a student athlete for others to look up to and aspire to become when they grow up.

DEVELOPING PROFESSIONAL RELATIONSHIPS

When I arrived at the University of Kentucky, I wanted to surround myself with individuals who would not only help develop my academic and athletic potential, but would also make me a better person in the process. New experiences help transform you from a teen into an adult during your first couple years of college. Having peers to help guide you along the way is essential to becoming successful in your future endeavors. One thing that will get you quickly stuck in sinking sand is to act as if you know it all and not be willing to listen to the advice your peers give you. It never hurts to be quick to listen and slow to speak when your peers are giving you guidance.

There were two professional individuals in my college career who were real difference-makers. One helped provide guidance towards matters relating to academics, and the other was a real motivator on the football field. I really feel blessed that they took time out of their busy schedules to offer kind words of encouragement and to mentor me along my college path.

The first individual is Bob Bradley, the Associate Athletic Director for Student Services at UK. At the time, he was the overseer of the CATS program. The CATS program was a real treasure for student athletes. It opened in 1981 and was the country's first academic center specifically created to cater to the student athlete. This facility offers computers, tutors, career counseling, mentoring programs and internships free of charge to the student athlete. According to the 1997 Edition of the University of Kentucky Football Media Guide, it was so successful from 1981 to 1997, "Kentucky has placed 171 players on the Southeastern Conference Academic Honor Roll, more than any other league school in that period."

From the moment I first met Bob Bradley, I knew that he was going to be a great mentor and an even better friend. He always had an open door policy and was willing to talk to me about academics and life in general. You could tell that he really cared about the student athletes at UK and wanted to see everyone succeed. I can still remember sitting in his office talking about investments and the kind of return a full scholarship football player could get if he invested one-half of his $40 weekend meal money in stocks or mutual funds. You would be surprised how much that type of investment would grow at an annual return of 8% over the course of four to five years.

The professional relationship that I enjoyed with Bob gave me increased confidence in where I was heading in my pursuit of a bachelor's degree in Finance. The road to success can be narrow for the student athlete who plays athletics in college, while striving to be successful in the classroom. It really made all the difference in the world to have someone to talk to who had seen so many student athletes pass through those doors at CATS. Some made the right decisions in their professional careers, and others did not take it as seriously because of their one-sided athletic dreams. Thanks to Bob, I feel like I made the most of my college academic experience.

The second individual is a person that I have already briefly talked about in Chapter 3 "The Anticipated Recruiting Process". He is Coach Ray Dorr, the recruiting coach responsible for getting me to attend the University of Kentucky. If ever a person had a real zest for life and enthusiasm for the game of football, Coach Dorr was that person. I remember one practice when the running backs were doing monkey rolls and Coach Dorr pulled one of the players out of the drill and took his place. He was everything you could ever ask for in a coach and more. There was always the element of surprise in what he was going to do next on the field to get the players excited about practice.

Coach Dorr was a good friend to me during my time at UK, and I will always remember him for seeing the potential I had at the middle linebacker position. He would always encourage me in the weight room and on the football practice field. He took his job seriously and looked out for the players that he recruited. He is the type of coach you really come to respect and appreciate during your collegiate athletic career.

These two professional relationships offered a balance to my life at college. They were mentors in the areas of academics and athletics and helped me successfully steer down that sometimes treacherous college path, a path full of crucial decisions to be made. College is much like the game of Monopoly. Make the right decision and you pass go to collect $200 dollars. Choose the wrong decision, and you go straight to jail. It may not seem realistic to compare the decisions a student athlete makes to getting a paycheck or going to jail. The truth is that I have seen student athletes succeed in college to enjoy lucrative and enjoyable careers in the business world. At the same time, I have seen student athletes make the wrong decisions and go to jail, due to check fraud, carrying a lethal firearm and public intoxication, to name a few things.

SPRING PRACTICE IN FULL BLOOM

My first semester at the University of Kentucky seemed to go by in the blink of an eye. It was a semester full of studying and scout team duties that often left me exhausted and ready for bed. If there was ever a good year to be redshirted, 1994 was definitely the year. The Wildcats won the season opener against their state rival, the Louisville Cardinals; however, they ended up losing the remaining 10 games of the season. The 1-10 record posted in 1994 was the worst since 1982, when they lost 10 games and tied one. Even though the Wildcats were playing in the Peach Bowl a year before, past results never hold any promise to future victories when it comes to football. That year the true freshman who were redshirted watched from the stands as their Wildcats yielded to defeat 10 games in a row. It was just the motivation to thrive on when it was time for spring practice to begin.

Although it was admittedly nice to be done with practices after a season that ended with 10 consecutive losses, there would be repercussions to be paid in the spring. There is not a college football team in the country that loses that many games and have the coaches just forget about it. Failure is something to build on, and being reminded of it presented not only an opportunity for personal growth, but also mental toughness.

Prior to the start of spring football practice, there was still the matter of spring conditioning that every college football player gets to experience for himself. I never really understood why, but somewhere along the college football conditioning path, it was decided that this conditioning would be done at six in the morning on Monday, Wednesday and Fridays. In order to give yourself sufficient time to start morning runs at 6 a.m., you would have to get up by 5:30 a.m. to get dressed at the Nutter Facility and walk over to the indoor facility. I can still remember waking up in the middle of the night and checking my alarm clock to make sure that I would not miss getting there on time.

Waking up that early can make a person do unconventional things. During my first experience with morning runs, there was one occasion where I got up at about 3 a.m. and got dressed to go to the Nutter Facility. For some crazy reason my body thought it was 5:30 a.m. and it was time to do conditioning. Once I got to the Nutter facility to change into my workout clothes, I was confused why the doors were locked. Luckily, the light bulb in my head finally turned on as I looked down at my watch and realized what I had done. I returned to the dorm to catch a couple more hours of sleep before I really had to wake up. Looking back, I always found it funny that my roommate did not say anything to me as I got up that early to get dressed and head over to the football locker room. You think he could have at least said something like, "Dude, where are you going at 3 a.m. in the morning?"

Morning runs typically consisted of a full hour of all out hustle. When the clock struck 6 a.m., if you were not in line ready to perform stretches before starting some serious conditioning, you were considered late. The players identified as being late would come to the indoor facility on a Tuesday or Thursday to do some special conditioning with a couple of the coaches. If you think a coach enjoys being at an indoor facility at 6 a.m., you had better think again. The coach's lack of enthusiasm for being there really translated into a conditioning session that you would not forget anytime soon.

After the players stretched for about five minutes, the team was broken up into two separate units. Usually the offensive players were in one unit, and the defensive players, in the other unit. One unit would go to a series of stations that were set up, and the members were broken up into position groups like linebackers, secondary, defensive ends and defensive linemen. These specific stations consisted of drills that lasted for about five minutes in duration. One of the least favorite drills I can remember was two 2 x 4's that were connected together forming a cross. This was set on the indoor turf and an orange cone was placed in the middle of the cross. Two players would position themselves directly opposite of each other in one of the slots created by the cross. When the coach blew the whistle, they would chase each other around the cone on all fours. Every time the coach blew the whistle, they would have to change directions.

There was a garbage can appropriately located close to this station because it was very common for players to lose whatever they had in their stomachs from the day before due to chasing each other around in circles. Other garbage cans were conveniently located throughout the indoor facility to accommodate players that had to vomit. This is the type of conditioning I am talking about here - conditioning the body to go past failure by doing what you did not think was possible. That is exactly what it takes to be a champion.

The other unit would report to the track and perform a series of forty 40-yard dashes and would have to complete each one in a specific period of time, depending upon what position they played. Once this group had successfully completed their running quota, the two units would swap from the stations to 40-yard dashes or vice versa. After both units completed both portions of the conditioning program, the sweet sound of the head coach's whistle would blow, and Coach Curry would gather everyone together to say a word about the effort given before dismissing the team.

Once morning runs were over, spring ball officially started. The conditioning was just a tool to get the body ready to have a successful spring practice. It is here that your position on the depth chart is determined, and the time to show the coaches that you have what it takes before reporting in the summer for doubles. The NCAA regulates the number of practices that a college football program can conduct in the spring. They are broken up into padded and unpadded practices and spring ball usually lasts about three weeks. The last official practice was the annual Blue and White Scrimmage held at Commonwealth Stadium and open to the fans.

Spring ball is a time to fine-tune your skills at your position and to mature as a football player. There are many football athletes who make it to the college level on instincts and talent alone. Spring ball is a springboard to really become a student of the game. For linebackers it means understanding your gap responsibilities and pass coverage responsibilities. The unique thing about the linebacker position on defense is that you are equally responsible for the run and the pass. You are called upon on every play, and there is no such thing as an off play. When you're the middle linebacker of a defense, your reading and passing along the defensive signals from the sidelines, calling the strength of the offensive formation to set the front four defensive linemen and reading any offensive clues to provide additional information to your teammates about the upcoming play. You are the quarterback of the defense, and you had better be ready to bring it when a fullback is running at you full speed or when you are called upon to blitz the quarterback at warp speed.

There can be no second guessing yourself, and you have no other option but to be confident in your abilities. If you are not, you are not going to be starting on Saturday afternoons. As hard as it is for me to admit it, a lack of confidence during spring ball was exactly my problem. In high school, I was successful on the field, and when I got to college, I was expecting the same results right away. The problem is that for most players, it does not happen right away. You have to be patient and allow yourself to mature as a player.

An opportunity to grow in what I like to call football maturity presented itself while we were watching the Blue and White scrimmage in our linebacker position meeting. This is where I knew that it was going to take some time to develop into the kind of college football player that I envisioned for myself. As we were watching the scrimmage film, the linebacker coach was going around the room telling everyone how many tackles they recorded. When he got to me, he said something like, "Viera, zero tackles." I replied by saying, "Coach, I didn't make one tackle." That is when he said, while eating his shiny red apple with a smirk on his face, "Nope, just a couple of J.O.P.'s." I said, "What is a

J.O.P. Coach?" After a moment of silence, he said, "Viera, that stands for 'Jump on the Pile'."

I was accustomed to making tackles in high school, but I could not even get credit for making one lousy tackle in our final scrimmage of spring ball! It was a rough first year in football, but quitting has never been a word in my vocabulary. I have a question for the college recruits reading this who are looking to embark on their freshman year. Is it going to get tough your first year of college? Without a doubt, you are going to be tested and pushed to your extreme limits. The question is, "Are you willing to stick it out and keep on pushing forward?" You have to believe that you are going to succeed, because if you do not, then you have already failed. I truly believe what separates a good football player from a great football player is not only skill and how hard they work, but maintaining hope in fulfilling their dreams and refusing to quit at all costs. Learning from the past and pushing ahead full steam was just what I planned on doing.

THE OPPOSITE SEX 102

How can I possibly talk about balancing your life in college and not bring up the opposite sex? Women take our breath away, and make us do crazy things, even though we pretend we are stronger than steel and faster than a speeding bullet. It is a wonder that some of us even find time to study while expelling so much energy pursuing the opposite sex! It is somewhat ironic that we can suit up on the field and clash helmets with other grown men, and at the same time, a woman can bring us to tears over a break-up. Women can fill our hearts with an overwhelming joy, and later in a relationship, make us feel like our hearts are going to explode into a thousand pieces.

There has to be a balance when it comes to this aspect of your life. You have to be mindful of your athletic and academic responsibilities while being involved in a relationship with a woman in college. Time is of the essence when you are a student athlete, and every minute is too indispensable to waste. You must learn to become proficient at managing your time when a female is a part of the picture. A woman can provide comfort and support in a meaningful relationship, but she can also become a distraction if you are only looking for a good time.

Now this is going to get a little personal for some of you, but I feel like this needs to be said. A woman is to be cherished and not simply used for your personal pleasure. God first created Eve in the Garden of Eden to be a companion for Adam, and not merely a sidekick that he could just treat any way he pleased. When God finished creating the Earth along with Adam, he knew that man would need a companion like nothing else already created. Therefore, God put Adam in a deep sleep and used one of his ribs to create His most magnificent creation. The reason I believe he used a rib close to Adam's heart is because of the special bond created in the heart of a man and a woman in marriage. It also shows that a woman is equal to a man and not above or below. God could have used Adam's ear or maybe even one of his toes but he chose a rib close to his heart.

When I attended college, it was very apparent that some football players were involved with women for only one thing. That one thing was a far cry from any sort of personal relationship. Plain and simple, they were looking for sex, and would be willing to say and do anything to get it. My dear friends, sex can be a double-edged sword and can be most easily compared to fire. In a marriage relationship, sex is like a fire in a fireplace. It is warm and comforting, and it is the way that God intended for a married couple to enjoy each other. When it is done casually and carelessly, it is like a wild forest fire that is out of control - burning and consuming everything in its sight, because its appetite cannot be satisfied and its thirst cannot be quenched. It is a decision that only you can make, and I would hope that student athletes and college students alike would take abstinence more seriously in college and life in general before marriage.

It really should not be a surprise to anyone why the divorce rate in the Unites States is over 50%. Casual sex is so mainstream in our society that it is hard to watch a television program or movie these days without some sort of sex scene or sexual innuendo. Some of the music broadcast over the radio and sold in records stores is certainly not helping the situation. Our society wants us to think that sex is okay outside of marriage and tries to condone it in the media with cover stories about celebrity romances and affairs.

Perhaps you came to college and have a girlfriend back home, or you have recently found a girlfriend at college. Maybe your girlfriend came to the same college to be with you. You might even be one of those guys who are currently flying solo in college. Whatever situation you find yourself in, the end result should be the same. Women you meet in college should be treated with respect and class. You should treat them the way you would like to be treated. Someone out there right now could be dating your future wife and hopefully they are treating and respecting her with class. Shouldn't we be doing the same?

SCHOOL'S NOT OUT FOR SUMMER

In high school, just about every student looks forward to the summer. I always picture the movie "Grease" when thinking about school being out for the summer. In the movie, the seniors at Rydell High have their last day of classes, and everyone comes running out of the school, screaming and throwing schoolbooks in the air. All of a sudden, a musical breaks out with John Travolta, Olivia Newton-John and all their friends, as they sing the "We Go Together" song at the school fair.

College football puts an interesting twist on your summers if you are serious about stepping it up and competing for playing time during the upcoming season. There is always the challenge throughout your college football career to continue to get bigger, faster and stronger during the off-season. The summer is probably the best time to make substantial progress in these areas. Due to players having a lighter schedule during the summer, there is more time for lifting weights, conditioning and eating everything in sight.

After completing my freshman year at the University of Kentucky, it was highly encouraged for all football players to stay on or close to campus for the summer football training program. One thing that should be pretty clear by now is that even though college football season starts in the fall, preparation for the players is a year-round responsibility and a full-time job. After having to drop Chemistry for two semesters in a row, I decided that it would be best to stay for summer school during the 4-week and 8-week sessions offered at the college.

Another perk about having a full scholarship is that your room, board and tuition are not only covered during the fall and spring semester, but also during summer school. The expenses that were incurred for my 4-week and 8-week courses were fully covered in my scholarship. In addition, every scholarship football player taking summer school received a monthly stipend of around $750 to cover living and food expenses - not a bad deal for staying at college during the summer.

Now if there was ever a course not to take during a 4-week class, it would be Accounting 201. The class met for two hours a day Monday through Friday, and there was a test every Friday. The amount of material covered during each week was mind-boggling, and by the end of the four weeks, I had nothing but debits and credits floating around in my head. Needless to say, it was nice when that last test came around and the course was complete. The two 8-week courses that consisted of Communications 101 and Economics 201 were a nice change of pace due to not having to meet everyday. An additional 4 weeks to go over the chapters allowed sufficient time to absorb the material being taught. After having a dose of a 4-week accounting class, that was the first and last time I took a 4-week course in my college career.

During my first summer at college, my roommate and I rented a very small, one-bedroom apartment close to campus that did not cost more than $450 a month. We were looking for somewhere not very expensive, so we could utilize the monthly stipend allocated to us. If you had walked into our apartment, it would not take you long to figure out why it was so cheap. The apartment basically had two rooms. The bedroom, living room and kitchen were all connected together and due to people liking to have privacy when they are taking care of their business; the bathroom was located in a separate room. For two college student athletes looking to save a little cash, it was the perfect place to stay for three months.

Besides the obvious studying taking place during the summer, there was still the matter of the conditioning and weight lifting for preparation for the upcoming football season. The man in charge of leading the Wildcats to getting bigger, stronger and faster during the summer went by the name of Hoss. The name designated to the strength and conditioning coach at UK was basically a synonym for "a really big dude." There comes a time in every football player's career when you have to give respect to someone because he deserves it. In the case of Big Hoss, the 20-inch neck and the fact that he squatted and dead lifted barefoot automatically created a high level of respect for the colossal-sized strength coach among the football players. Everyone loved having Hoss in the weight room pushing us beyond our limits.

During my first year at UK, I remember when the basketball players had Midnight Madness at Rupp Arena to kick-off their new season. At the same time, some freshman on the football team decided that it would be cool to have a Midnight Madness of our own in the football weight room. After several freshman, including myself, decided they were up for the challenge to lift during the middle of the night, Big Hoss (whose heart was even bigger than he was) met us at the weight room after midnight. The heavy metal music was blasting on the gym radio, and the freshman players who showed up got after it like never before in the 20,000 square foot gym. Working out in the middle of the night was a memory that I knew would never be forgotten, especially after seeing Big Hoss jumping in the Mosh Pit that a couple of the players created. The big man truly was a kid at heart as he let the players push him around in the Mosh Pit in a lighthearted fashion. You could tell he not only loved his job, but also really cared about his football players.

There did not seem to be as many players staying for the summer during the 4-week summer school session. The summer training program during this period of time consisted of basically lifting four times a week and light conditioning. It was during the 8-week summer school session that summer training really started to intensify and heat up. Lifting in the weight room was very intense during this time due to the fact that every player had a customized workout. The workouts would require you to lift more weight each week based on your three-set max taken on the bench, squat and power clean in the spring. The more weight you lifted for your three-set max on these exercises in the spring correlated to pushing even more weight in the summer.

In addition to the heavy lifting, the summer conditioning program was geared to prepare the players not only for the upcoming football season, but also for the run test that had to be completed by each player when they reported to training camp in August. The run test was a series of sprints that had to be completed in a specified period of time based upon the position you played. For example, offensive linemen would not be expected to run as fast as cornerbacks or wide receivers, so their time would be adjusted accordingly.

Preparation for this run test and the upcoming season consisted of a wide variety of cardiovascular conditioning exercises. There were the obvious conditioning exercises like running sprints and running the mile in a specified period of time, but more importantly, I was introduced to the type of conditioning that could really take a player to the next level. It was during this summer that I ran stadium steps in the midday heat of July like never before. Stadium steps in a high school stadium are one thing but when you are in a stadium that holds close to 60,000 screaming fans, that is a totally different experience. There were also sprints with parachutes and sprints that were run while wearing a harness with grip handles that another player would hold onto to offer you resistance. There were even shuttles we ran as our midsections were encircled in a giant rubber band that would sling us back to the starting point after stretching it to capacity.

It was a different world of weight lifting and conditioning that I was exposed to that summer as I participated in the 8-week summer training program. My body responded well to the physical activities that had to be completed in the gym and under the sweltering summer sun. I felt primed and ready to report to training camp, weighing a very solid 225 lbs. With a year already under my belt, I was anxious to see how the new season would unfold. This season there were no plans to watch the games from the stands, but to be an active participant and make my mark on UK football. I desperately wanted to hear "Viera" called out in Commonwealth Stadium for making a tackle, and nothing was going to stand in my way. In my mind, it was time for all the hard work to pay off.

I'M A TRAVELING MAN IN A PROGRAM OF CHANGE

Change in a person's life is as inevitable as having to get out of bed in the morning. Sometimes you just want to lie there, but eventually you get out of bed and face the reality of a new day. This is similar to change in a person's life because once you are confronted with a changing environment, you might want to avoid it or even pretend it is not happening. Sooner or later, you eventually have to face the music. The redshirt freshmen who were ready to embark upon their second official year of college football would be exposed to a changing environment that they never could have foreseen prior to signing college football commitment letters in high school.

After the completion of a season that ended in a 1-10 record, there had to be changes on the offensive coaching staff. The pressure from alumni and fans alike resulted in offensive coaching changes that were probably already in motion upon the completion of the prior year's season. The defensive coaches remained intact, but there was a new offensive coordinator, Coach Elliot Uzelac, on the scene from a college called Colorado University. He was the offensive coordinator at Colorado when reputable players like Kordell Stewart, Charles Johnson and Eric Bienemy were lighting up the scoreboards. In addition to the new offensive coordinator, there was also a new running backs coach from Navy. Hopefully these coaches would provide the plays and discipline needed to rejuvenate the offense to being a scoring threat in the SEC.

A change that no one anticipated was when our beloved Hoss had to relinquish his duties as strength and conditioning coach for the football team and provide his services to other athletic sports like baseball, soccer and tennis. The big man got a raw deal, and we missed having him work with us during the '95 season. The new strength and conditioning coach, Rob Oviatt, came from Oregon State and brought with him an assistant strength coach, who was a nutrition specialist for the players. It was difficult saying goodbye to Hoss but I must admit the new weight training staff did an excellent job with the football team that year. Coach Oviatt was very precise in his training regimen for the players and the team made impressive strength gains under his strength and conditioning program. He was also a coach that cared about his players and really understood the demands student athlete's face in academics and athletics.

After a busy off-season spent getting stronger and faster, the defense was expected to step it up a notch during the '95 season by providing the offense with the turnovers needed to create scoring opportunities. It was also expected to do a better job of limiting the opposing team's offense to minimal yardage and points scored. It was clear in doubles that nothing less than 100% effort on the field would be accepted by the defensive coaching staff. Pursuit drills had to nearly be perfect so that they did not have to be repeated. There seemed to be an intensified focus by the defensive coaching staff to make up for the previous season.

Doubles in the summer of '95 were the hottest that I can ever remember having during my college career. It was in the mid 90's everyday, and some days seemed to push 100 degrees with the heat index in the Bluegrass State. After each practice, players would be lined up, waiting to submerge themselves in bathtubs full of water and ice to help revitalize their aching muscles. In addition, we were drinking three to four metrix shakes after each practice to supply our bodies with the extra calories needed. The Russian shower was introduced to us that year, and it became a staple after every practice. For those of you who have never heard of a Russian shower, it consisted of turning the water as hot as you can bear on a sore muscle like your legs or back for a short period of time. After doing this, you simply turn the water as cold as it will go, and have the water hit the same aching body part. This would shock the body, due to the extreme temperature change in the water, and your body would recover faster.

It was a crucial time for players to listen to the advice given by the training staff to avoid cramping on the field or in the locker room. Water fountains were placed wherever players were located on the practice field, and they were encouraged to drink water as often as they could. Even though multiple steps were being taken by the training staff to prevent dehydration, players were still cramping up in high numbers. It was so bad that numerous athletes had to be given IV's to replenish fluids lost on the practice field. It was like a scene out of the sitcom, "M.A.S.H," when you walked into the training room. Every table had a player sitting on it with an IV.

There were two incidents relating to cramping during '95 doubles that stick out in my mind for one reason or another. The first was when a wide receiver whose locker was close to mine cramped up right there on the locker room floor with nothing on but his bath towel. The trainers had to come into the locker room to massage and ice down his legs before he eventually was given an IV. The second incident was when the team was listening to Coach Curry talk to us in the main meeting room before one of our double practices. One of the defensive linemen cramped up right outside the meeting room doors prior to the start of the team meeting.

As Coach Curry talked to us, the trainers attended to the big defensive lineman, but the cramps were only getting worse. This was evident to the players and coaches alike, as the defensive lineman yelled out a long string of profanities that would make even a sailor blush. Coach Curry tried to continue with what he was saying, but had to take a short break, due to the vulgar language coming from the defensive lineman right outside the meeting room doors. Everyone felt bad for the defensive lineman, but there was just something funny about the way the big man cursed about those cramps. One thing was for certain about those cramps, and that is that they were certainly a curse for our team during '95 doubles.

At the end of doubles, I found myself at third string on the depth chart for the middle linebacker position. There were two upperclassmen in front of me who had college game experience, but I was second string on almost every special team. Being third string was disappointing after working so hard during the summer, but I was excited about being able to suit up with the team during the games and about the prospect of getting some playing time on special teams. Unless there were injuries at the middle linebacker position, I knew my chances of playing time there were pretty slim.

My goal of not watching the games from the stands became a reality in the '95 season. The only problem was that instead of the stands, I was watching the games from the sidelines. The first game of the year was against our in-state rivals. The Louisville Cardinals came to town, and there was not an empty seat in Commonwealth Stadium. Our football team stayed at one of the nicest hotels in Lexington on Friday night to get prepared for the big game the following evening. Every player who dressed for the game was issued a Wildcat warm-up outfit manufactured by none other than Nike. The dinner Friday night was catered by the hotel and consisted of steak, chicken and more steak. The food being served was absolutely incredible. It was not the most important thing I should have been focusing on, but it was hard not to notice, with steaks piled so high they almost looked like they were going to tip over.

That evening the linebackers met with our linebacker coach/defensive coordinator, and we went over the opponents tendencies with regard to down and distance, reviewed formation recognition and went through the different signals that would be coming in from the sideline. After eating a snack that was delivered before bedtime, it was lights out until the following day. The worse part about having an evening game is the anticipation. The whole next day consisted of eating breakfast and lunch while going in and out of either position meetings or team meetings. When it was finally time to head over to the stadium, it was done first-class all the way. The players got on the luxury buses and were police-escorted to the stadium from the hotel. Not too many people can say they have had a police escort somewhere, unless of course, they were being arrested for something or rushed to the hospital.

That night the Wildcats played a tough game, but in the end the Cardinals won by a score of 20-14. It was the first of many games that season where I would be a spectator instead of a playmaker. In spite of having to watch the games, week in and week out, I prepared as if my name would be called out onto the playing field. The reality was that I was still only a redshirt freshman. My patience was going to have to persevere, even though it was certainly being tested. Somehow, I knew deep down inside that in the end, it was all going to come together spectacularly and that I was going to be a great college linebacker.

Many college players do not get their break until they are juniors or seniors in college. The hardest part about this whole process is that you perform the same amount of preparation for the games, but can only watch your teammates from the sidelines as they play under those football lights. You are in essence an understudy for a brilliant or not-so-brilliant actor, and are waiting for your chance to shine in front of the anxious and excited audience. The problem is that not all actors break a leg or get sick before their big performance so you could be waiting for a while.

It was a season of waiting as the two linebackers ahead of me performed on the field week in and week out with only minor injuries. Even more amazing, almost the whole season went by before I was finally called to play in my first official college game on special teams. That season we traveled to Indiana, South Carolina, Georgia, Mississippi State and Vanderbilt. As we played the Bulldogs in Starkville, the special teams coach said, "Viera, get ready because you are going in." Much to my dismay, it was only a false alarm, because the player in front of me did not need anyone to substitute for him. By this point, I was ready to jump out and tackle the other team's ball carrier if he came close to our sideline with the football.

Usually the players with less experience (or in my case, none) get to play in college games when the end of the game is near, due to the score being out of reach. The problem our team had was that we were rarely in the lead, and always seemed to be playing catch-up to our opponent. When you play teams like Florida, Auburn, LSU and Tennessee, there is little room for error. It was not until the second to last game of the season that I finally stepped onto the field at Commonwealth Stadium against the Cincinnati Bearcats. It could not have been more than two to three plays on special teams during that game, and from what I remember, I was just trying to hit somebody on the other team before the referee blew his whistle. One play was spent trying to get up off the ground due to a Bearcat jumping on top of me after slipping on some mud.

Those were my only highlights for the 1995 Wildcat season, and it certainly was not anything I was going to brag about. The Wildcats followed up the 1-10 previous season with a dismal record of 4-7. The season had its share of highlights like our star running back running for 429 all-purpose yards in a victory over the South Carolina Gamecocks. We even had our share of close games like almost beating Peyton Manning and the Tennessee Volunteers before losing 31-34. Like the old saying goes, "close only counts in horseshoes and hand grenades," and football was not in either of those categories. We needed to win games and everyone could foresee more coaching changes being made prior to the following season.

As other redshirt freshman players played enough quarters to receive their letterman jacket after the completion of the dismal 4-7 season, I was left with a bitter taste in my mouth wanting so much more from the upcoming season a year away. Why couldn't I have lettered that season? Why were things so difficult when I was trying so hard? Looking back now, the answer to those questions is that I just was not ready. You might be saying, "Ready for what? All you do is run around and play the game." My dear friends, college football is much more than just a game, it is an institution of physically gifted athletes who are a step away from taking it to the next level. The fact is that I just had to patiently wait my turn to shine in the spotlight like the players before me who went through the same waiting game. Hindsight is always 20/20, but when I had all these feelings and emotions running through me, at the time it was hard to try to make sense of it all. A very small taste of playing that year

WALKING ON HIGHER GROUND AND AWAKENING THE SPIRIT WITHIN

would be all I could take with me into another off-season.

CHAPTER FIVE

THE BIGGEST DECISION YOU'LL EVER MAKE

For God so loved the world that He gave His only begotten Son that whoever believes in Him should not perish but have everlasting life.
- JOHN 3:16

Therefore, if anyone is in Christ, he is a new creation; old things have passed away; behold, all things have become new.
- 2 CORINTHIANS 5:17

I am the light of the world. He who follows Me shall not walk in darkness, but have the light of life.
- JOHN 8:12

WALKING ON HIGHER GROUND AND AWAKENING THE SPIRIT WITHIN

Suppose you ask your good friend, "What is the biggest decision you will ever make?" What do you think they would say? For some I suppose it might be what college they decide to attend, where they choose to work their first job or even who they will marry. I wonder what you would say has been the biggest decision in your life. For me, it has been accepting my Lord and Savior, Jesus Christ, into my life. It is a decision so powerful and moving that it not only has earthly ramifications but also determines your eternal fate.

This decision completely changes your outlook on life as you know it, and lets you see the world through the eyes of Christ. It is a world that for the most part is living in the darkness of time, while the light of the world shines in a select few. It does not take much more than turning on your television to see how far our society has come to take away the "shock and awe" factor that existed when I was growing up in the 80's. The sad thing about our society today is that there are few things that really shock us anymore. Topics like sex and homosexuality were rarely discussed and now programs centered on these matters can be found on your television 24/7. The latest and greatest reality shows like "The Bachelor" or "Joe Millionaire" are centered on sexual innuendos, while watching an episode of "Will & Grace" or "Queer Eye for the Straight Guy" will expose you to more homosexuality than you can stand.

Some of you have no idea what I am talking about while others are completely tuned in to every word I say. My goal is for everyone reading this book to know the steps that need to be taken to be able to receive Jesus Christ as their Lord and Savior. From there, it is solely your decision to make. In the previous chapter, we discussed different ways to juggle academics, athletics and a social life. Having Jesus Christ in your life is by far the most important part of finding a balance in college life. He not only grounds us, but lets us know the difference between right and wrong. Make no mistake that Jesus is the solid rock on which we all should stand in our lives. Any foundation other than Jesus is just unstable ground.

So maybe you are asking yourself, "Why did he not bring this up in the previous chapter?" That is a very valid question. The truth is that I did not receive Jesus into my life until the spring of my redshirt freshman year in college. Prior to that, I thought I had it all figured out, but before we go into the specifics of the most important decision I have ever made, we first have to go back to the beginning.

TO BE OR NOT TO BE RELIGIOUS? THAT IS THE QUESTION.

Not long after I was born on February 4, 1976, my parents had me baptized at our local church. As long as I can remember during my childhood, every Sunday, my brother and I attended church with our parents. After service, we would get to go to the convenient store and pick out either a pack of baseball cards, football cards or some type of sugary, sweet candy. There was nothing wrong with a little reward for behaving well at church! In the first grade, I received the "Bread of Life" for the first time and took required religious classes at the private school we attended. The reason I am telling you all of this is because what I am about to tell you is coming from a person who grew up in the church.

Looking back on my time spent in our local church, there were many good memories. I enjoyed getting to hear God's word from the Bible with my parents and brother. The time spent at our private school provided me with a disciplined way of life, which helped me decipher the difference between right and wrong. It also provided me with some excellent penmanship skills. The area of concern I have with the church we attended was the blurred and unstable presentation of the gospel on Sundays, and I had no idea of what it meant to be saved. Those are two pretty enormous negatives, when you consider not being saved translates into an eternity spent away from heaven. The meaning of a personal relationship with Jesus Christ was foreign to me and utilizing the gift of the Holy Spirit was relatively unknown and unspoken of in our church.

Our congregation believed you get to heaven by being a good, moral person. It was okay to merely know who Jesus Christ was and the thought of inviting Him into your life was not discussed or encouraged. This is a tough, rugged world we live in, and I want to be frank with you about this topic. After all, it is dealing with your eternal life after your physical life on this earth comes to an end. The devil and his demonic angels go to church and know who the Son of God is, but the Holy Bible does not say anything about their going to heaven anytime soon. As a matter of fact, in the end the Lord will ultimately defeat them because he is the "Alpha and Omega."

If a person agrees good works is all that is required to enter heaven, they would also have to agree the Bible is not 100% accurate. The reason I say this is because Ephesians 2:8-9 contradicts that assumption when it says, "For by grace you have been saved through faith, and that not of yourselves; it is the gift of God, not of works, lest anyone should boast." The very grace of God is what allows us to be saved. There is nothing we can do to earn it because the price has already been paid on the cross. Romans 10:9-10 says, "If you confess with your mouth the Lord Jesus and believe in your heart that God raised Him from the dead, you will be saved. For with the heart one believes unto righteousness, and with the mouth confession is made unto salvation."

The God we worship is the God of second, third and fourth chances. All sins are forgiven when you accept Jesus Christ as your personal Savior; however, the Bible tells us there is one "Unpardonable Sin." Jesus tells us in Matthew 12:31, "Therefore I say to you every sin and blasphemy will be forgiven men, but the blasphemy against the Spirit will not be forgiven men." What is Jesus trying to tell us here? If the only way we can receive the Holy Spirit is to receive Christ, then by not professing Christ as your personal Savior, you are denying the Holy Spirit. The one unforgiving sin is not receiving Jesus into your life.

The religious frame of mind is exactly where I was when I first started college as I was praying the Lord's Prayer every night before I went to bed. I even read the Bible and prayed to God everyday. The problem was that I had a religion instead of being a Christian. You might be asking yourself what the difference is between being religious and being a Christian? I wonder how many people think those two things go hand and hand. In the world we live in, it seems like just about everyone in college says something like "You must be religious if you don't drink beer."

There are about as many different religions out there as there are flavors of ice cream and many of them are worshipping false gods. Christianity separates itself from any other religion because of one simple truth. In Billy Graham's daily devotional titled "Unto the Hills", he says, "Christianity is not a religion. It is a relationship with a living God. Jesus, Son of God the Father and Second Person of the Trinity, is the central figure of our evangelistic message." This personal relationship is what differentiates the life of a Christian from someone who is merely immersed in religion and not carrying on a personal relationship with their Lord and Savior, Jesus Christ. "For there is no distinction between Jew and Greek, for the same Lord over all is rich to all who call upon Him. For whoever calls on the name of the Lord shall be saved" (Romans 10:12-13).

TAKING SALVATION PERSONALLY

As I was getting acclimated to the college environment my first two years on campus, I was also getting involved in different organizations outside of football. It was nice interacting with the players on the team, but I also wanted to mingle with the student life. During one of my many classes at UK, a student invited me to attend an evening meeting with an organization called Campus Crusade for Christ. This is a Christian outreach organization led for the most part by the students on college campuses across the United States. They are committed to reaching students with the gospel of Jesus Christ. It is also an excellent way to meet and have fellowship with Christians on campus.

When I first started attending these meetings, it was a little strange to see how happy everyone was acting. I did not consider myself a "kill-joy," but I also did not walk around with a smile on my face from ear to ear for no reason at all. Besides, I was a football player and we were supposed to be tough, right? The meetings I attended on Wednesday evenings had a live band that sang Christian songs, involved skits with students who dealt with college life situations, and included a message from the gospel given by the speaker. Reflecting back on this time, it was very uplifting and encouraging being around other Christians with the same ideals, who wanted to live a life that was pleasing to Jesus Christ.

From the time I attended these meeting from my freshman year in college to my redshirt freshman year, I heard the sinner's prayer at every meeting. I watched countless students say that prayer to receive Jesus Christ in their lives. That is not only a praise to Campus Crusade for Christ for their ministry but a bigger praise to Jesus for reaching lost students through this organization. It was in the spring of my redshirt freshman year that the very essence of the sinner's prayer touched my soul. One night the light bulb in my head finally turned on during one of those Campus Crusade for Christ meetings, and I realized what it meant to have a personal relationship with Jesus Christ. As I went back to my dorm room, I pondered my salvation, realizing that I had never prayed that prayer. As soon as the door closed in my dorm room, I was down on my knees on the side of my bed, praying that Jesus would come into my life.

That night I proclaimed to Jesus that I believe He is the one and only Son of the Almighty God. I affirmed that Jesus was born of the Virgin Mary through holy conception and that he lived a flawless life on this earth, not committing even one sin. Not only did I acknowledge that he died on the cross so that my sins in the past, present and future would be forgiven, but that through my belief in Him, I would be promised eternal salvation in heaven when my life on this earth comes to an end. What a wonderful feeling it was to know that I now had a personal relationship with my Savior! All my sins had been forgiven, and my eternal fate was sealed and secure in heaven. That was the day my name was written in the Book of Life in heaven because I made the decision to accept and give my life to Jesus Christ.

Have you ever prayed this prayer? If you haven't I encourage you to pray it right now. If there is one thing in life that I want to be 100% certain about it is my eternal salvation. This prayer is so easy to say, but so many people are not willing to give their lives to Christ. I think the reason something so simple can be so complicated for many people is because the last thing the Devil wants you to do is receive Jesus in your life. Once you make that personal decision, you are entitled to a first-class ticket to heaven instead of riding in coach to hell. Many people think they can push this decision off until they feel like they are at the right place in their lives. The problem with this type of thinking is that no one ever promises us another day on this earth. Who says we'll even wake up tomorrow morning or not catch some kind of sickness in the blink of an eye? Our health is something a lot of us take for granted. We live in a society where we think we can handle things on our own, but in the end, we always fall flat on our faces. The truth is that everyone needs Jesus Christ in their lives. That might not be what some of you want to hear at this stage in your life, but it is what you need to hear.

Romans 3:23 says "For all have sinned and fall short of the glory of

God." Just like when God created Adam and Eve and walked with them in the Garden of Eden, we all need to personally walk with Jesus Christ. Romans 6:23 goes on to say "For the wages of sin is death, but the gift of God is eternal life in Christ Jesus our Lord." He is the only bridge to our Heavenly Father in heaven.

It should be crystal clear in 1 John 1:9 when John says, "If we confess our sins, He is faithful and just to forgive us our sins and to cleanse us from all unrighteousness", that Jesus wants us to come just as we are. He desires to have a personal relationship with you and has the power to forgive you of all your sins. You could not ask for a better friend. Regardless of who you think will never let you down in life, there is only one person that can hold up to that promise and that is Jesus Christ.

Coming to the Lord with all of my imperfections was exactly what I did that night in my dorm room. Some of you might be thinking, "How can Jesus possibly forgive me for the sins I have committed in the past?" That very question was answered for every sinner when Jesus died on the cross for our personal sins. He was the ultimate sacrifice so that we would be saved. As we examine who Jesus claimed to be, there can only be one right answer. He was either the Son of God as he proclaimed, or he was simply one confused individual. The problem with our society is that too many people want to say that Jesus was a good, moral prophet who sort of fits in between the two scenarios like a piece of turkey between two slices of bread, but not the Son of God. How can you proclaim to be the Son of God if you are not and be a good and moral person with such an outlandish claim? Jesus above all proved who he was by rising on the third day to defeat and conquer death.

When I think of my belief in Jesus Christ without seeing what the apostles saw, I always think of what Jesus said to the doubting Thomas. The other disciples saw Jesus before Thomas after He rose from the grave. Thomas simply did not believe them, and said he would not unless he could see Jesus for himself and physically feel the nail marks in his hands and the hole in his side from the spear that pierced Him. I wonder how many people reading this book feel like Thomas that they need more proof that Jesus is truly the Son of God. Eight days passed after Thomas's remarks, and Jesus appeared before the disciples and Thomas. Jesus told Thomas, "Reach your finger here, and look at My hands; and reach your hand here, and put it into my side. Do not be unbelieving, but believing"

(John 20:27). Thomas simply did all he could do at that point and said to Jesus, "My Lord and my God" (John 20:28). The part that comes next is what keeps my faith stronger than ever. After Thomas's acknowledgement that Jesus was the Son of God, Jesus says, "Thomas, because you have seen Me, you have believed. Blessed are those who have not seen and yet have believed" (John 20:29). Blessings are certainly abundant for those of us who believe in the Son of God without seeing the miracles he performed with the apostles and his triumphant victory over death. The sad thing is that the very people who saw Him in person are the same people who had Him crucified on the cross, instead of choosing a common thief.

THE POWER OF THE HOLY SPIRIT

The testimonies of those who have received Jesus as their Lord and Savior are all unique and different. Many people make radical lifestyle changes because they realize that what they were doing in the past was not pleasing and respectful to God. The lifestyle of others may not have been as extreme prior to receiving Christ in their life, but waking up every morning still takes on a whole new meaning when you know you have secured a first-class ticket to heaven. If we look in the New Testament, there are countless examples of people who changed their ways after making that personal decision. The person who has always stuck out in my mind was Paul, formerly known as Saul.

If ever a person in the New Testament despised Christians, Saul was definitely that someone. It says in Acts 9:1-2, "Saul still breathing threats and murder against the disciples of the Lord, went to the high priest and asked letters from him to the synagogues of Damascus, so that if he found any who were of the Way, whether men or women, he might bring them bound to Jerusalem." Saul not only did not like the Lord's disciples; he despised them so much that given the chance, he would kill them. Out of all the people Jesus could have chosen to spread the gospel, He chose someone who persecuted and killed Christians. The very reason I think He chose Saul is because He wanted to show us how having Jesus in our lives can transform and change even the darkest villain.

The story of Saul's conversion took place as he was walking on a road to Damascus on a journey to persecute Christians. As he was approaching Damascus, thinking about what he was going to do to those Christians that he so much despised, Acts 9:3 says, "Suddenly a light shone around him from heaven." At that very moment Saul fell to the ground and was blinded by the light. That light that shined so brightly that day was the very light of Jesus Christ. In Acts 9:4, Jesus says, "Saul, Saul, why are you persecuting Me?" After Saul inquired as to whom this blinding light was that caused him to fall down, Jesus told Saul that it was the very person he was persecuting. Blinded and afraid, Saul asked the Lord what it was that He wanted him to do. Jesus then told him to go into the city, where everything he needed to know would be told to him.

Saul was blind for three days and without food or water before a disciple called Ananias was chosen by Jesus to visit Saul. The purpose of the visit was to accomplish three things. Ananias was to restore Saul's sight, allow Saul to be filled with the Holy Spirit, and finally, to baptize him. Once these three things were completed, Saul almost immediately became an unstoppable force, preaching the gospel of Jesus Christ everywhere he went. Today the New Testament is filled with stories about Paul (formerly known as Saul) and his God-inspired writings, which continue to encourage fellow Christian believers all over the world.

The story of Paul has always been encouraging to me because the day I received Christ in my life, I spent the next month reading completely through the New Testament. It was there that I really started to understand how Jesus can use anyone to spread the gospel. If he completely changed the life of a villain who killed Christians, how much more can He change our lives? You see, Jesus doesn't go out and look for the qualified to do His work, because everyone falls short of His glory. He takes the unqualified and through His grace, makes them qualified.

As I was beginning to understand my new faith in Jesus, I started to learn about the gift of the Holy Spirit that dwells inside of us after we receive Christ in our lives. The Holy Spirit is what helps us to really decipher between right and wrong. Just because you become a Christian doesn't mean that everyday is going to be sunny and bright. It also doesn't mean that we are going to live perfect lives from here on out. I think a general misconception of unbelievers is that they think Christians live perfect lives and never do anything wrong. To clear up that misconception the only perfect person to live on this earth was Jesus Christ. Besides, it was Jesus that told Paul in 2 Corinthians 12:9 that "My grace is sufficient for you, for My strength is made perfect in weakness."

My journey in faith brought me a greater understanding of taking care of my body as I read 1 Corinthians 3:16 that says, "Do you not know that you are the temple of God and that the Spirit of God dwells in you?" Although I didn't indulge in alcohol before becoming a Christian, I became more aware of how I was taking care of my body spiritually, mentally, physically and nutritionally. After all, with the Spirit of God taking residence inside of me, I wanted to live a life that was respectful and responsible to my Heavenly Father. This is always a challenge when living in a college environment, and it proved to be wise to spend my free time with other Christian friends.

SPRING BREAK VS SPRING BALL

If I had to choose whether I liked spring break or spring ball more in college, I would have to say spring break. There is no comparison between tackling grown men wearing football equipment and lying on the beach, soaking up warm rays. The latter is definitely more relaxing while the tackling is just plain exhausting, but extremely fun in its own sort of macho way. The first trip I took in college for spring break was with Campus Crusade for Christ. It was a mission called "Outreach on the Beach" in Daytona Beach, FL. I remember a long van ride from Lexington, KY to Daytona, but it was well worth the trip. There is something special about the beach. The ocean breeze gently whistles past you as you walk in the sand, and the smell of the beach makes you want to stay out all day long.

Although it was spring break in Daytona, students from all over the country involved with Campus Crusade for Christ were meeting at a fellowship hall every morning and worshiping the Lord together. It was a special time, seeing so many students with the same belief as I have in the Lord Jesus Christ. Our mission on this trip was to evangelize to the lost on the beaches of Daytona. There was a small pamphlet that we read from to explain to others about the price that Jesus paid on the cross so that our sins would be forgiven and that we would be able to spend eternity, with Him in heaven. I'm embarrassed to say that I did not share the gospel with more than two or three people that week. It was not an easy task for me, because although I recently received Christ into my life, it was difficult to talk to strangers about Him. It felt awkward and it was probably the unknown reactions from sharing the gospel that scared me the most. What should have scared me more was missing opportunities to share the gospel of Jesus Christ with unbelievers. Looking back, I cannot think of anything scarier than spending an eternity separated from God. The reason I'm sharing this is because I think that as you progress in your faith, sharing the gospel becomes easier to do. Besides, you're really just telling people about your new best friend in Jesus Christ.

The trip to Daytona lasted a week, but the memories of the fellowship with other Christian believers will last a lifetime. It was a great experience that prepared me to take a leap of faith. I was ready to be a shining light to others in college and motivated to tell football players and friends alike about the personal relationship I enjoyed with Jesus Christ. More importantly, I really wanted to tell them the steps they could take to enjoy the same type of relationship and firmly secure a place in heaven. It felt like God brought me to Kentucky for a reason, and while I was there, I needed to tell my teammates about the love Jesus had for them.

Once we got back from spring break, it was morning runs all over again at 6 a.m. I made it a point to run when I was on spring break so that when I got back to Kentucky for spring conditioning, I wouldn't have heavy lungs. The extra work paid off, and after morning runs were complete, I felt more than ready to get it going on the football field. During the spring of '96, I felt like a new man. My love for football seemed to grow stronger than ever because of my relationship with Jesus Christ. After all, everything that I did from here on out was going to be solely to glorify Him. It was Philippians 4:13 that I took with me into spring ball, "I can do all things through Christ who strengthens me." That was my battle cry that spring, and I knew that with God for me, there was no one I could possibly fear.

During our allotted number of spring practices, I continued to learn and excel in every practice. There was one spring practice in particular that I remember. I knocked an offensive center on his back during one on one drills while Coach Curry watched close by. Later, in the same practice, I picked off three passes from our two quarterbacks as they were trying to complete passes in skeleton drills. The effort and results on the field were being noticed by the coaches and by the end of spring ball, it earned me the number two spot on the depth chart at middle linebacker. I was behind the junior starter from the previous season, but that spring I graded out the highest of all the linebackers. Our linebacker group that year went by the name of "Old School LB's". We were leading the way to bring together the "Big Time D-Line" and "The Old Dirty DB's" to form a ferocious, tenacious and relentless defense that wanted to make a name for itself. The future looked bright and I gave all the glory to my Heavenly Father.

THE POWER TEAM PACKS A HEARTY PUNCH

It was during the spring that a Christian strength group called the Power Team made their way to a church in Lexington, KY for three days of bone crushing feats of strength. My roommate, Big Mike, heard about them coming to town on the radio, and we decided to go check them out. It only took one trip to realize that these guys were the "real deal." Sure, they did the usual things like rip phone books, tear license plates in half and break Louisville Slugger baseball bats over their knees (which Big Mike tried to master after attending each show), but they also performed other feats of strength you would have to see to believe.

Some of these amazing feats of strength included running shoulder first through several blocks of ice and breaking cinder blocks that were on fire with nothing but a small towel wrapped around the striker's hand. My personal favorite was when a member of the Power Team ran full speed down the church aisle before smashing into a 2 x 4 chest first, which resulted in the wood exploding into several pieces.

So you are probably asking yourself, "Why in the world would these grown men subject themselves to such punishment?" That is an excellent question. The answer is simply because they were doing it to give all the glory and honor to their personal Savior, Jesus Christ. You see, after these feats of strength were performed, they would explain where they got their strength from and the relationship each of them enjoyed with God's perfect Son. Before the show was complete, they asked everyone to bow their heads and if someone never accepted Jesus into their life and wanted to make that decision, all they had to do was raise their hand.

After Big Mike and I attended the first show, we vowed to gather together as many football players as we could find to watch the Power Team the following night. The next day came and despite sharing our enthusiasm with the other players, we were able to get only two teammates to join us. As we watched the show, it was just as amazing and incredible as the night before, but what happened next still vividly lives within my memory. The speaker once again asked everyone to bow their heads and asked if anyone wanted to invite Jesus into their heart. As our eyes were shut, little did I know that the two players we invited both raised their hands to receive the gift of eternal salvation. As I raised my head and opened my eyes, I suddenly felt the power of the Holy Spirit tug at my heart, and a couple of joyful tears streamed down the side of my face. To my surprise, I was watching my first roommate at the University of Kentucky walk down the church aisle to talk to the counselors about the decision he had just made to receive Christ into his life

Later that night I talked to him about the decision he made and told him how happy I was for him. He asked me if I wanted to know why he had made that decision at the end of the show, and I certainly was interested to find out. He told me that when the speaker asked if anyone wanted to receive Jesus, he looked over to me to see if I had my hand raised. He knew the life that I lived and because I did not raise my hand, he wanted to experience the same relationship with Christ that I enjoyed.

The reason I wanted to share this story is because you can never assume that your friends are not watching you closely. I tried to be a shining light to my first roommate, and to God's glory, a seed planted early in his college career was watered that night and sprouted a brand new Christian. Needless to say, the Power Team was an unforgettable and memorable ministry to witness in person that spring.

LEAVING IT ON THE PRACTICE FIELD

The successful completion of my sophomore year at college was followed by a month of much needed rest and relaxation at casa de Viera. There is no place like home when you are living in a dorm room. Home cooked meals and nothing to do but exercise was just what the doctor ordered. After getting to spend a month with my parents in Cleveland, it was back to the University of Kentucky to take two classes for an 8-week session of summer school. One of the major benefits of taking summer school classes while staying in an apartment by campus is that classes are not only free, but you also get the monthly stipend for living expenses. I figured taking two classes would be better and easier on the body than working a summer job and then having to do summer conditioning and lifting.

There was a good turnout of players who stayed for the summer and completed the scheduled workouts and conditioning drills. You can always tell that a player is serious about the upcoming college football season when he makes the commitment to stay at college for the summer. Knowing that I finished spring ball at the #2 spot at middle linebacker, it was time to kick it up a notch and make great strides in my strength gains over the summer. By the end of the 8-week training regimen for the football players, I was weighing about 225 lbs, tripled 385 lbs on the bench, squatted 475 lbs four times and power cleaned around 285 lbs. It was the strongest I had ever been, and the Holy Spirit inside of me was alive and kicking. Notice I said, "Holy Spirit," and not "Steroids." I have seen players travel down that dark road, which has always resulted in broken promises and unfulfilled expectations. Steroids are best known for wreaking havoc on the well-being of the human body. It is in essence short-term gains for long-term side effects. I encourage you to feed off the Holy Spirit for long-term gains and eternal well-being.

Now I was licking my chops to get a shot at banging helmets with the Louisville Cardinals for the first game of the season, but there was a small thing called doubles to take care of. This doubles was very different from any other I had participated in during my college career, mostly because I was getting a huge amount of reps during practice and my fair share of practice time with the first team defense. It was another hot summer, and when you are hot and tired, you sometimes do crazy things. One thing I remember vividly during those couple weeks of intensely hot practices is that the portable john was located on the other side of the practice field. With all the water we were drinking just to try to stay hydrated, it wasn't uncommon to make a trip over there two to three times during practice. There is nothing worse than being hot and sweaty while having to try to bypass your practice pants, girdle and jock strap just to go to the bathroom.

During one doubles practice that was almost hotter than you could stand, one of the defensive lineman let me in on a little secret. The theory behind the secret was that with all the water we were drinking, it was almost as clear coming out. This led us to the assumption that when our bodies were ready to dispose of the water, the pee was more like water with a little sodium. As we kneeled on the sidelines, waiting to get called into action, we did our business right there on the side of the practice field. The usual course it took was right down the leg and into the old football shoe. The funny thing was that we were so sweaty you couldn't even tell. I guess it was just one of those things that you have to experience for yourself to understand. To this day, my wife never lets me forget that I used to pee in my football pants in college.

THE CARDINALS COME TO TOWN

After an exhausting doubles prior to college classes starting, it seemed like everyone on the team was just plain worn out and tired. We had the Louisville Cardinals in less than a week but I knew my body didn't feel as good as I hoped it would before the first game of the season. I knew that doubles were not supposed to be easy, but it would have been nice to have had a few practices with just our helmets and shoulder pads to help rejuvenate our bodies. There is a fine line during doubles when it comes to excessive full contact practices. Coaches want to make sure that their team is sharp and prepared for opening day, but also rugged and tough enough to physically dominate their opponents. That summer, our team seemed to be teetering on that fine line.

The night finally came at Commonwealth Stadium, and there was not an empty seat in the house. The game was broadcasted on ESPN, and that definitely added to the excitement. I was on just about every special team and number two on the depth chart behind the senior starting linebacker. The butterflies were churning in my stomach that evening during the whole first half of the game. My parents and head football coach from high school were in the stands waiting for me to get my big chance. I got on the field for special teams, which was nice, but I knew the real action was at linebacker. I was excited and nervously waiting for the linebackers' coach to call my name, but before I knew it, the first half was over, and we were headed to the locker room.

I can't recall the score at halftime, but I can honestly say that I will never forget what happened on the field during the first play of the second half. The Wildcats were receiving the ball, and I was on the kick-off return team. As the ball was being kicked off to our returner, I ran back to form a wedge with some other players to offer protection for our return specialist. Before I even got the opportunity to block one of the opposing players, one of our Wildcats drove one of the Cardinals right into my left knee. The force was so great that it knocked me to the ground, and to my surprise I felt an immediate loosening of my left knee like a rubber band snapping. As I got up to run off the field, there was definitely something wrong with my left knee. I could still jog but something just didn't feel quite right.

As I approached the sidelines, I went directly over to the bench. After I flagged down the head trainer, he took a look at my left knee. He lifted my knee pad and proceeded to put one hand on my knee and the other on my calf. As he moved my knee to the left something very strange happened: My knee would not lock when he pushed it to the left. It simply kept bending sideways. It was an easy diagnosis, and I was told that it appeared to be a 3rd degree tear of my Medial Crucial Ligament (MCL). I remember asking him how long I was going to be out, thinking it could not be more than a couple of weeks. When he said at least 8 weeks, for a second, I thought it was all just a bad dream. With only ten games left in the season, I would be lucky to play the last two against Vanderbilt and Tennessee.

After the diagnosis of my left knee, I was put on a motorized cart and driven to the locker room. I remember riding on that cart, looking over to my teammates on the field, and seeing them raise clenched fists in the air, as if they were going to continue to battle for me. There was an immense feeling of disappointment that I experienced; knowing that I could not be with them, competing for the Governor's Cup. It was a humbling and devastating experience, after spending so much time and energy getting ready for the 1996 football season. Later during the second half of the game, I came back on the field sporting crutches and a brace on my left knee. All I could do was watch the outcome of the game that ended in a score of 14 points for the Wildcats and 38 points for the

Cardinals. The season was just starting, and so was my road to recovery.

LEARNING TO LEAN ON JESUS

It really is just a matter of time before a football player experiences an injury either on the football field or on the practice field. The game is just too dangerous to stay healthy during your career and that is a risk that all football players are willing to take. It is what makes playing football special and why everyone is not willing to participate. It is not a big secret that football is a very physical game but sometimes the physical part sneaks up on you and results in an injury. Players are taught that every play could be their last and that if they continue to hustle on the field until the whistle blows, it will help them avoid getting injured.

The time finally came in my career to sustain an injury that would temporarily sideline me from the game that I loved. I have always tried to be an eternal optimist and try to look at my glass as being half full instead of half empty. I realized that I was very fortunate to not have torn my Anterior Crucial Ligament (ACL) (which not only would have required surgery, unlike an MCL injury, but also would have taken at least 6 months of rehabilitation). The final diagnosis of my injury after a trip to a knee specialist resulted in six to eight weeks of rehabilitation before suiting up to practice. The most important thing I had going for me was that I now had Jesus in my life to lean on for encouragement and a great family to support me during the next eight challenging weeks of rehabilitation.

During my knee rehabilitation, I remember receiving an encouraging card from one of my four roommates that were living with me in a rental home close to campus. It is hard to remember exactly what that card said but what I do recall very clearly was this passage from Psalm 23:1-4,

> *The Lord is my shepherd; I shall not want. He makes me to lie down in green pastures; He leads me beside the still waters. He restores my soul; He leads me in the paths of righteousness For His name's sake. Yea, though I walk through the valley of the shadow of death, I will fear no evil; For You are with me; Your rod and Your staff comfort, they comfort me.*

It is amazing how God works in our lives. That was exactly the passage I needed to hear at that point in my life. There was nothing to fear and I knew that Jesus was going to take care of me. I truly believe that Jesus speaks to us through not only reading the Bible, meditating on His Word and our prayer life, but also through acts of kindness shown to us by our friends, family and even strangers. Jesus was speaking to me through that encouraging card and letting me know that if he takes care of all the flowers of the field and trees of the forest, he would provide for me even more. We were created in God's likeness and His Son Jesus desires to have a personal relationship with us. For in Matthew 10:30-31, Jesus says, "But the very hairs of your head are all numbered. Do not fear therefore; you are of more value than many sparrows." Who else can love us or know us better than God? He is so intimately familiar with us that God knows how many hairs are on our head. What an awesome God!

As I meditated on Psalm 23, I started to feel comforted and began thinking about the story of Job in the Old Testament. This story talks about a man named Job who was very blessed by God. After a debate between God and Satan in heaven, God decided to test Job's faith by giving Satan permission to turn his life upside down as long as he didn't kill him. As soon as Satan was given the okay, he didn't waste much time and Job's life almost immediately changed in the blink of an eye. It probably took less than a minute for four messengers to reach Job almost instantaneously to tell him that all he had had been destroyed by a series of random events. That even included losing all his sons and daughters. After hearing the devastating news from the messengers, it says in Job 1:20, "Job arose, tore his robe, and shaved his head; and he fell to the ground and worshiped." What a great example of a Godly man. It didn't say that he cursed God for losing everything but he merely fell to his knees and worshipped his Heavenly Father. Job goes on to say in Job 1:21, "Naked I came from my mother's womb, And naked shall I return there. The Lord gave, and the Lord taken away; Blessed be the name of the Lord."

This story hit home for me because Job realized that God was sovereign in his life. He knew that everything that happened to him was reviewed by God first. This acknowledgement of God's sovereignty resulted in Job being blessed with more than he had before he endured his trials. I realized that God had a purpose for me injuring my knee and instead of dwelling on my injury, I needed to start focusing on the recovery.

That is just what I did week in and week out for the next eight weeks. I was required to stay on crutches for 4 weeks without any knee movement. Even though I had to crutch to my classes around campus, I was fortunate enough to get a handicap parking pass. God provided for me in my time of need and I'm proud to say that I didn't miss a class during my rehabilitation process. After 4 weeks of using crutches, it was another four weeks of building the strength back up in my left knee. I really think the home-cooked meals provided by my mom on weekends my parents drove down to visit helped provide my body with the additional nourishment and encouragement I needed to keep me going strong. The worst part of the whole process was definitely getting back my flexibility due to the scar tissue that built up during the healing process. After more trips to the training room than I can count, it was the week before the last game of the season against Tennessee before I was given the green light to suit up for the practice field. Eight weeks felt like a long road to recovery, but I was really grateful that the injury was not as serious as it could have been.

PEYTON AND THE BOYS

The Wildcats had four wins and six losses as we were getting ready to head into Knoxville to take on Peyton Manning and the Tennessee Volunteers. Even though our season record was dismal at best, the game was still a big rivalry. The game was expected to have an attendance of over 100,000 screaming fans. After a solid week of practice and getting back into the swing of things with my bulky knee brace on my left knee, I was excited to travel to Knoxville. I was put back on special teams and with the game being broadcasted on ABC; it was a great chance for my family to watch me play on television.

The day of the game finally came and I still remember stepping into the biggest stadium in the country at that time. The capacity at Neyland Stadium in 1996 was 102,544. That day there were 102,534 fans in attendance. It was incredible to hear the roar of a crowd that size!

Regardless of whether or not the Wildcats won the coin toss, one thing was for sure that day. After eight weeks of rehabilitating my left knee, I was going to step on that field with either the kick-off team or the kick-off return team.

The Wildcats won the toss and decided to kick the ball off to the Volunteers. As I was getting ready to sprint down the football field, my nerves seemed to be going everywhere at once. The noise from the sea of orange and white was almost deafening and as our placekicker kicked the ball off I found myself running as fast as I could go. It would be nice to say that I made my first collegiate tackle on that play, but I didn't. As a matter of fact, the returner for the Volunteers was quickly approaching me, and as I committed to going one way, he simply went the other. The Tennessee game gave me the opportunity to step on the field plenty of times, with the Volunteers scoring 56 points to the Wildcats 10. When you are getting beat by more than 40 points, games tend to last longer than if you are the one winning.

It was finally the last couple of minutes of the game, and my name was called to play middle linebacker. It was the moment I had been waiting for since I came to Kentucky. As I sprinted on the field to play against a young Tee Martin, who would later lead the Volunteers to a national championship, it was there that I recorded my first of many collegiate tackles. Our linebacker coach might as well not even have called any plays from the sidelines, because my mind was blank as soon as I stepped on that field. I had to rely on my instincts to take me to the ball. The signals were being called from the sidelines, and it seemed like it was the first time I was seeing them. Feeling rushed on the field to get the defensive linemen in position each play, I blurted out something that might have sounded like 50 shade, and got ready for the ball to be snapped. It wasn't my best performance, but a tackle is a tackle. It might not seem like a big deal to some people, but for me, it was a monumental stepping stone. It felt like the monkey finally jumped off my back. After the game was over, the Wildcats lost, but I felt as if I had achieved something far greater than a victory that day. I learned to persevere through a difficult season and end it with a high note. It was one of many tackles that I would make for Jesus and one of many occasions that I would give him all the glory and honor.

CHAPTER SIX

SHOULD I STAY, OR SHOULD I GO?

Ask, and it will be given to you; seek, and you will find; knock, and it will be opened to you.
- MATTHEW 7:7

All our fret and worry is caused by calculating without God.
- OSWALD CHAMBERS

Jesus Christ is the same yesterday, today, and forever.
- HEBREWS 13:8

The last thing a college student athlete wants to think about is the possibility of having to transfer to a different college. Depending upon how long you stay at your first college, there are comforts that continue to grow throughout your college experience. There are obviously the friends that you meet in the sport you play and the classes and extracurricular activities you attend. The overall familiarity of the campus that you walk around everyday grows with each day that passes. Let's not forget about the relationships that can develop between you and your coaches and peers. For many of us, there is even a "significant other" at home or close to campus. It is never easy to think about having to leave these comforts behind and starting all over again.

Whether or not you are faced with the decision of having to transfer to another college, you should at least know the process that is involved. If you are a freshman, next time you're in a team meeting, I want you to take a good look at your fellow freshman teammates that signed to play at the same college. Over the next four to five years, those faces that you get to know so well through doubles, football seasons, spring ball, strength and conditioning programs and college classes will slowly disappear. Some college athletes will not make it academically, others will simply quit the team, some might get arrested and put in jail, and there are those who will eventually become unhappy with their situation and transfer to another college. It is uncommon these days to have more than 10 to 15 players left your senior year after starting out with a freshman class of around 25 players.

Deciding to transfer to another college is nothing short of a huge decision. It is a decision that will alter the course of your life. You'll undoubtedly meet new friends, develop some lifelong relationships with coaches and peers along the way, either love or hate the old or new state you go to college in and maybe even meet your future spouse. That is quite a bit to take in when thinking about making just one decision.

My hope is to take the fear out of this decision if it is one you are faced with in college. I want you to be fully equipped to make an educated decision about continuing your education and collegiate athletic career if you become unhappy with where you are attending. Life is too short to be miserable during college. After hearing my story about the transfer process, perhaps it will shed some light on your situation. There is a lot to cover in regard to the transfer process, so get something to drink and maybe even a couple of snacks, and let's tackle this together.

A NEW COACHING STAFF COMES TO TOWN

The 1996 season for the Wildcats ended in another dismal record of 4-7 for the second year in a row. After the Wildcats' first seven games of the 1996 season tallied a record of 1-6, it was announced during the week of the Georgia game that our head coach, Bill Curry, would be fired at the end of the season. It was confusing to the players why the University did not wait until the end of the season to make their announcement but the news was used as fuel for the Wildcat players. The next three games against Georgia, Mississippi State and Vanderbilt were hard-fought, emotional victories for our head coach. After the Tennessee loss at the end of the season, the University was already well into the recruitment process of finding a different head coach for our football team.

There were mixed feelings among the players about the upcoming change in the overall football coaching staff, but decisions made at that level were beyond our control. All the players could do was hope for the best. Besides, a different coaching staff was a fresh start for all the players, and everyone would be working hard toward earning a starting position on the field for the upcoming 1997 season. It might just prove to be the competitive spirit this team needed to turns things around in the SEC.

After several months of recruiting, the decision was made to hire a head coach named Hal Mumme from a Division II college called Valdosta State. The head coach compiled an impressive record of 40-17-1 during the five years he spent coaching at Valdosta State, and his fun and gun offense was something that seemed to be a good fit for our highly touted sophomore quarterback, Tim Couch. The news reached the football team that this decision had been made - not by the former Athletic Director at the University at that time, but by watching a local news station. It seemed strange to learn about our next head coach at the same time the greater area of Lexington did. The players were glad the search was over, and wanted to focus on preparing for the upcoming season.

When the new coaches arrived in Lexington, things started to change quickly for some players before spring ball even started. Our starting quarterback, Billy Jack Haskins, had already transferred to a Division I AA college called the University of Rhode Island prior to the start of the second semester, due to the coaches' intent of starting Tim Couch, regardless of the outcome of spring ball. Multiple linebackers, including myself, were moved from the linebacker position to defensive end and other players were switched from offense to defense or vice versa. When a team gets different coaches, you should expect to be moved around. After the position changes, I was willing to see how spring ball went before I made any immediate decisions about what the future would hold.

PRAYING FOR A MUCH NEEDED SIGN

Regardless of how hard I tried to learn and enjoy playing defensive end for the Wildcats during our spring practices, it was just not going well. I had been playing middle linebacker since the 4th grade and when you go from being the quarterback of the defense to a three-point stand on the defensive line, it can tend to be a difficult transition. Spring ball came and went, and I could see myself going from starting linebacker during the upcoming 1997 season to the 3rd string defensive end. It was not exactly what I had in mind for my redshirt junior year. Although I was still unhappy with football, I continued to pray to my Lord and Savior, Jesus Christ, for guidance and stayed in Lexington for summer lifting and conditioning.

It has always been hard for me to have a bad attitude when the Lord had blessed me with so much. Even though at that time I was a defensive end, I was very grateful that I was also a reborn Christian. I spent a great deal of time that summer reflecting on the more important things in life like eternity in heaven, the forgiveness of my sins, and being filled with the Holy Spirit. I wanted to be a light in this world and have other players be drawn to me, so I could share the gospel of Jesus Christ with them. I wanted to partake in the Great Commission that Jesus talked about in the New Testament and lead others to Christ by being a fisher of men. That summer my relationship with my personal Savior continued to grow as I prayed about my future at the University of Kentucky.

Doubles started up once again in the summer of '97 and after a week of the usual hustle and bustle I found myself as the 3rd string defensive end playing on the scout team against Tim Couch and the 1st team offense. Many of the players on offense were guys that were in my freshman class four years ago. I felt embarrassed to be playing against them on scout team. My heart kept telling me I should be starting at middle linebacker. After much fervent prayer to my Lord and Savior to give me a sign as to what to do, I made the decision to ask the linebacker coach/defensive coordinator why I had been moved from the linebacker position to defensive end. The linebackers that had been moved the previous spring were never told why by the coaching staff. You would think after spending four years of your life playing for a University, they could have at least told you individually why they decided to change your position.

It seems like only yesterday (although it has already been eight years) since my Lord and Savior gave me the sign I prayed for so earnestly that summer. After being frustrated during doubles for almost a week, I finally went up to the linebacker coach/defensive coordinator after the completion of our second practice that day and politely asked him why my position had been changed. I also asked him why I was never given the opportunity to compete at the middle linebacker position. The coach simply told me that I was too slow and could not flip my hips. I guess the good thing about the explanation that I got was that it was straight to the point; however, I wasn't buying it one bit. I knew from that instant that I would never again be given the chance to play middle linebacker at Kentucky. The problem was that I knew I could do all things through Christ and really felt like I was destined for great things on the football field. If it wasn't meant to be at Kentucky I would just have to go somewhere else.

Later that evening when the players were eating dinner at the cafeteria, as if I needed more of a reason to initiate the transfer process, the head coach called me over to the table he was eating at with some other coaches. He asked me what I asked the linebacker coach/defensive coordinator as if I had done something that personally insulted him. I told him that I was just curious why my position had changed from middle linebacker to defensive end during the spring. That is when he repeated what the other coach had said about being too slow and not being able to flip my hips, as if I had forgotten what the other coach had told me earlier in the afternoon. He reminded me how lucky I was to have a full scholarship and that it wasn't guaranteed for the duration of my stay at the University of Kentucky. He proceeded to call me a cry baby like many of the other upper classmen and said that if I didn't want to be part of the football team that he would be happy to allow me to transfer to another school. It was a nice little chat between me and the head coach that night; however, little did he know that he just answered my prayer.

When you pray to God for an answer, you should expect him to come through in a big way. After all, He is the one and only Creator of the Universe. There is not a prayer too big or too small that God can not answer. I'm not saying that it is going to be the answer we are always looking for in life. Jesus knows us better than anyone, which means He also knows what is best for us. My Heavenly Father made it very clear to me that it was time to initiate the transfer process. The sign I had prayed for that summer was signed, sealed and delivered. After talking to my parents that night, the next day, I went up to the head coach and told him that I would like to take him up on his offer and allow me to transfer to another college. I must say that he was a man of his word, and I really felt like it was God leading me somewhere else to do his work and play middle linebacker in the process.

THE PATH TO WISDOM & KNOWLEDGE

There is a story in the Old Testament about King Solomon that reminds me of the most important thing I prayed for during the transfer process. This goes far beyond praying for a sign so I knew it was time to transfer or even praying that the Lord would provide me with a college that wanted to offer me a full football scholarship. Now after Solomon, the son of King David, was anointed the King of Israel for the second time, he was given the opportunity to ask God for anything. The story takes shape in the second book of Chronicles where Solomon went up to the high place in Gibeon. He was making one thousand burnt offerings to the Lord on the tabernacle of meeting throughout the day. It says in 2 Chronicles 1:7, "On that night God appeared to Solomon, and said to him, Ask! What shall I give you?" Can you imagine what it must have been like for Solomon to be able to ask God for whatever his heart desired? He could have asked for riches, power, popularity or anything else under the stars. In 2 Chronicles 1:9, Solomon says, "Now give me wisdom and knowledge, that I may go out and come in before this people; for who can judge this great people of Yours?" Solomon could have had anything, but he simply asked the Lord for wisdom and knowledge. That is exactly what I was praying for during the transfer process. I knew if I was granted that prayer, everything else would fall into place.

The reason I was so confident that things would be taken care of is because after Solomon asked for wisdom, the Lord tells him in 2 Chronicles 1:11-12, "Because this was in your heart, and you have not asked riches or wealth or honor or the life of your enemies, nor have you asked long life - but have asked wisdom and knowledge for yourself, that you may judge My people over whom I have made you King - Wisdom and knowledge are granted to you; and I will give you riches and wealth and honor, such as none of the kings have had who were before you, nor shall any after you have the like." You see, the Lord ended up giving Solomon all the other things anyway because of his request for wisdom and knowledge. I'm not saying that I was looking to get rich and powerful. I simply knew the Lord would provide for me during this time in my life and guide me along the way.

After I decided to transfer to another college, I picked up my belonging in the UK football locker room and said goodbye to the players for the last time. It was hard knowing that I had spent over three years with these players and developed great friendships before having to say goodbye. They all wished me well and knew that it was something that I had to do. I think that some of them even wanted to come with me. I remember as I was walking out of the Nutter facility that the head coach made a comment to me that I didn't need to be hanging around and distracting the players. I guess it was his strange way of wishing me good luck in my future endeavors.

Prior to telling the head coach that I wanted to transfer, there was a little homework that had to be done. As I was initially thinking about the transfer process during spring ball and into the summer, there were questions I wanted answered before I made my final decision. I needed to know whether all my college credits were going to transfer, whether I would have to sit out of football for a year and most importantly, who was going to offer me a full scholarship this late in the season, especially after coming off of a 3rd degree MCL tear a season ago and having very little college playing experience to my credit. It worried me that we were already going on our second week of doubles, and the 1997 season was only two weeks away.

Besides praying to God for wisdom and knowledge during this process, I had to meet him half-way and make some calls. The first person I called was my head coach, Bob Lake, at Cloverleaf high school and talked to him about my situation. He was going to make some calls for me to Villanova University and Boston University to see if they would be interested in a transfer linebacker this late in the summer. He also told me that if I transferred to a Division I AA school that I could play right away and would not have to sit out for a season if I did not transfer to another Division I school.

After calling Coach Lake, I got the phone number for Billy Jack Haskins at the University of Rhode Island to discuss the transfer process with him that he had gone through just a semester ago. He told me about the colleges he was looking at and that the University of Rhode Island was the best fit for him. Besides Billy Jack, they also had a running back transfer from Clemson and a linebacker from West Point. He proceeded to tell me that all his credits transferred which was good news for me because at Kentucky, he was also in the business school. The best news came when he told me that they might be interested in another transfer linebacker from a Division I school, and he would talk to the head coach, Floyd Keith, for me.

I started to feel like all my questions were getting answered after talking to Billy Jack. Later that day, I had a sit-down discussion with my mentor, Bob Bradley, and explained my situation to him. I told him that I felt that I could obtain a quality education at another school similar to UK but what my current college could not offer was the opportunity to compete at the middle linebacker position. He understood my situation and said he would call around and see what he could do. With a G.P.A over 3.4 in Finance, he felt that Ivy League schools like Harvard or Yale might not be out of the question.

You can really see the importance of developing relationships with coaches, peers and players when you consider the transfer process. After talking to only three people, I felt very comfortable that something was going to develop according to God's plan for me. The same day that I packed up my belongings in the UK locker room and said my goodbyes, it was time for God to answer another prayer. That would be providing me with another college to transfer to for my redshirt junior year. That answered prayer came when Billy Jack Haskins called me back the day after I decided to leave the UK football program. He said the head coach at URI was very interested in talking to me on the phone. I want to be very clear that at this time the required written permission to transfer from UK had been obtained before I spoke to the head coach at URI. The NCAA has very strict rules about contacting another college before written permission is obtained from your college to transfer. After a long discussion with the URI head coach on the phone, he wanted to offer me a full scholarship. If that is not an answered prayer in a time of need I don't know what is. The amazing thing is that they offered me a full scholarship without even watching any game film. They simply took Billy Jack's and Coach Uzelac's word that I was a quality linebacker.

The timing could not have been any better because they started doubles a week later than Kentucky. After talking to another one of the URI coaches regarding my college credits, I found out that every single one of them would transfer over to URI. That means I would not be required to retake any college classes. The Lord more than provided for me that summer as things fell into place during the transfer process. I verbally committed to URI over the phone and in less than a blink of an eye, I was Rhode Island bound.

JESUS TALKS TO ME IN THE MOUNTAINS OF PA

It is amazing how fast you can pack up and move when time is of the essence. The sooner I got out of Lexington and made my trip to Rhode Island, the sooner I could start practicing with my new teammates during doubles. After I verbally committed to URI over the phone, it was not more than a couple of days before all my belongings were packed into a U-haul truck and I started driving towards Cleveland with my car attached to the U-haul car dolly. My plan was to make a pit stop at my parent's house in Cleveland to unload my furniture and other big items before driving straight to Rhode Island. The trip to Rhode Island from

WALKING ON HIGHER GROUND AND AWAKENING THE SPIRIT WITHIN

Cleveland was a good 10 hours and I just wanted to take what I absolutely needed for college.

The drive to Rhode Island was exciting if you are a fan of traveling on the open road like I was during college. My trip would take me through Kentucky, Ohio, Pennsylvania, New Jersey, New York, Connecticut and then Rhode Island. Once I dropped off the big items at my parent's house and returned the U-haul truck and car dolly, it was not long before I was back on the road.

During my long drive to Rhode Island, I was filled with an inner peace about my decision. At the same time, I was excited about the opportunity to go to another college to get an education and play football. That inner peace I was experiencing came to an abrupt stop when I reached the middle of Pennsylvania. That is when the weight of the decision that I had made started to make me think twice about what I had done. On the one hand, it was very exciting to be traveling to a different state I had never been to before, to start fresh with football at the linebacker position. I would have the opportunity to take new finance classes at a different business school and make new friends all over again on and off the football field.

On the other hand, the farthest I had been east prior to this trip was Philadelphia, during my recruiting trip to Villanova University. Rhode Island was well east of Philly and so small that you could exit the state in any direction in about 45 minutes. I had received a full football scholarship from the University of Rhode Island without their even watching any game film, but the fact was I had accepted the scholarship without even having seen the school. What if the school was not all it was cracked up to be and I made a mistake? What if playing football at Rhode Island did not work out as well? It was amazing how fast these thoughts had rushed into my mind and really made me contemplate the decision I had made.

Not long after I started to think these thoughts, I put my faith into practice. I suddenly did what I wish I would do more often when life seems to get too overwhelming for us to handle. I prayed to Jesus that everything would work out just fine. It was a simple prayer, but I knew that one way or another, Jesus would give me an answer. Believe it or not, it was not more than a second after I had prayed in my car, en route to Rhode Island, that a small sign nailed to one of the many trees on the side of the road seemed to appear out of nowhere. The sign only had two words on it but they were exactly the two words I needed to hear. The sign simply said "Trust Jesus". To this day, I do not believe that sign was just a coincidence. It was much more than that. It was not only an answered prayer, but it was the Father's way of talking to me and letting me know that everything would work out just fine. It was then and there I knew that Jesus had a specific purpose for my transfer to Rhode Island. I could not wait to find out just what it was He wanted me to do besides play football and get an education.

NEW LINEBACKER ON THE BLOCK

After a solid 10-hour drive through six states, I rolled into Kingston, RI, around two o'clock in the morning. There was a football coach waiting for me under the athletic sign by a sports building called Memorial Coliseum. Once I introduced myself to the coach, he escorted me to the dorm room I would be staying at during football doubles. Before we even got to my room, I remember him knocking on one of the doors in the dorm, and two coaches came out in their boxers to welcome me to the University of Rhode Island. Even though it was two o'clock in the morning, you could tell they were excited to have me at URI. The next thing I knew I was laying on a bare mattress in a dark dorm room. I fell asleep in the clothes that I had worn on my long trip.

The wake-up call the next morning came from one of the coaches at about 6:30 a.m., so it was not exactly a good night's rest. To tell you the truth, I had a hard time sleeping that night, anyway, because I was excited to start playing linebacker again. One of the first players I saw when I went to the early breakfast that morning was Billy Jack Haskins. It was good to see at least one familiar face. I can remember the players asking me what position I played, and when some of the other linebackers found out I would be competing with them for playing time, you could tell that things were going to get a little competitive.

It had been over a year since I had played linebacker due to being moved to defensive end during the prior spring so there was a little rust that needed to be sanded. I must say that not having to get into a 3-point stance was definitely welcomed with open arms. The Rhode Island Rams had already been in doubles for a week once I arrived, so I needed to grasp the understanding of how the defense operated in a relatively short time. There was another week of doubles to go and then a week of practice before the Maine Bears came to Meade Stadium.

The Rams already had three starting linebackers when I arrived but they were willing to move one outside linebacker to defensive end so I could fill that spot. There was definitely some uneasiness about what had happened with that player's position, considering he was a senior and had played outside linebacker the previous three seasons. I could definitely relate to his situation seeing how I had come from a program that did something similar to me. All in all, he was a great sport about it and was really a team player that season. That type of sportsmanship really showed me what kind of players we had on this team. The Rams football players were a bunch of guys who worked hard together for the common goal of winning games. They took me into their team right away, and to this day I still keep in touch with many of the former Rams players.

MAKING EVERY TACKLE COUNT FOR JESUS

When the Maine Bears came to town after the first week of college classes, I finally had the chance I had been waiting for my whole collegiate career. There was a starting spot for me at outside linebacker, and I was going to make the most of my opportunity. The middle linebacker position at the beginning of the season was being filled by a senior player considered to have a legitimate shot at the NFL after the season was over, so I had to be patient for my turn as the quarterback of the defense. The other thing I had to be patient about was waiting a year to get to wear number 40 on the field again. This number was currently taken by a senior defensive lineman who had one of the coolest last names I have ever heard on the football field. When you hear the last name Konasavage you tend to think of somebody ferocious and violent. Many football players like to keep the same jersey number throughout their high school and collegiate career. The reason I think this is so important is because it is like a source of identity. When you hear "Number 40 on the tackle" over the speaker phones in stadiums season after season, it just doesn't have the same ring to it when they say "Number 46 on the tackle." The closest thing I could get to number 40 was number 46, so I went with it.

The first game against the Maine Bears started out with an explosive effort from our quarterback Billy Jack Haskins and the URI offense as we went into halftime leading 14-10. The second half was a different story as the Bears held our offense scoreless and scored 20 unanswered points to win 30-14. As if losing the season opener wasn't bad enough, our all-conference defensive end, Frank Ferrara, broke his leg on the second play of the game and would end up missing the rest of the season. This was my official college day debut as a starting linebacker, and even though we lost that day, I posted 8 tackles.

There is something special when you have Jesus in your life and you get the opportunity to play football or any other high school or collegiate sport. Regardless of what position you play or what your stats are at the end of the game, you have the opportunity to do it all for the Lord and give him all the glory and honor. Before each game I played as a Rhode Island Ram, beneath my shoulder pads was a shirt I wore that said "I will not be denied". This shirt was a reminder of what I had been through to get to start at the linebacker position and how I had persevered through my early college years. In addition, as I taped my wrists with athletic tape for extra support, I would write Philippians 4:13 on one taped wrist and on the other it would say "The Lord is with me; I fear nothing." Philippians 4:13 has always been my favorite verse in the bible and with the Creator of the Universe on my side, my heart and soul felt like the sky was the limit. Jesus brought me to Rhode Island for a reason. As I played each game that season, I would not only give Him all the glory and honor and play through the strength of the Holy Spirit, but more importantly, use this opportunity to witness to other players about a personal relationship with Jesus Christ.

Some people might look at a linebacker and say that he is just making a tackle in a football game. The fact is that every tackle I made during my collegiate career was for the one and only Jesus Christ. This was done out of reverence for His sacrifice on the cross so that not only my personal sins would be forgiven and the gift of the Holy Spirit would come upon me but that when I die, I would be given the opportunity to spend eternity in heaven with Jesus. We are saved by grace and nothing else. There is nothing we can do to earn our way into heaven. There are some who believe baptism seals your soul with Christ but it really is just a proclamation of your faith to other believers. All Jesus requires is that we surrender our lives to Him and have faith. He lived the perfect life for you and me and that deserves our whole heart and not just part of it.

WHAT HAPPENED TO THE SPARK?

During the beginning of every new football season, teams around the country play the first couple games hoping to establish continuity with their offense, defense and special teams. The first couple of games are so crucial because if you can ignite a spark on your team then it has a chance to turn into a fire and before you know it you're burning up the opponents on the scoreboard. There was no reason for the Rams not to be a quality football team with a transfer quarterback from Kentucky, a transfer running back from Clemson and a transfer linebacker from Kentucky. The fact is that when you play football, the team is only as strong as the weakest link. If ten players are taking care of their responsibility on the field and one fails to accomplish this, then you end up having something like a quarterback sack or the opposing quarterback burns your defensive back for a touchdown. The Rams just did not seem to work as a team on the field in 1997. One main reason was that we were decimated by injuries. The other reason was that we just could not finish games.

Although we won our second game of the season against Jerry Azumah and the New Hampshire Wildcats 35-21, we lost the next two games of the season against Northeastern 13-41 and Massachusetts 14-18. In the Massachusetts game alone we lost our starting quarterback, Billy Jack Haskins, to a separated shoulder, our second string quarterback to an ankle sprain, and one of our starting linebackers. The team was falling apart with a record of 1-3 and when Hostra came to town and won 28-21 we were faced with a record of 1-4. We were desperate for a victory to try to gain some momentum as we were about to approach the second half of the season. We headed to Boston University with a focused determination to accept nothing less than a victory and in the last minutes of the game our junior placekicker booted a 29-yard field goal to edge us past the Terriers by a score of 20-17.

A record of 2-4 was not pretty with only five games left but it was much better than being 1-5. If we could only put together back-to-back wins, maybe we could create that spark we had been looking for and ignite it into a flame. The wind must have really been blowing, figuratively speaking, the last five games of the season because we did not win one game. Losses to Brown, Connecticut, Villanova, Richmond and James Madison in triple overtime resulted in a dismal season record of 2-9 under head coach Floyd Keith.

There were four close games that season that were lost by eight or fewer points. If we had won those, we could have finished a respectable 6-5. It was simply a season that was not meant to be. There were some positives that came out of the 1997 Rams football season. I finished the season with 132 tackles, which led not only the team in tackles, but also the Atlantic 10 conference. During the middle of the season, I was moved from outside linebacker to middle linebacker and really found myself a home there. The middle linebacker who was there prior to me was moved to defensive end where he posted an impressive 10 quarterback sacks that season.

My first season at URI was about laying a foundation to build on for the upcoming 1998 season. That year I was chosen as Second-Team All-Atlantic 10 Conference linebacker and honored as the team's outstanding defensive back by the URI coaching staff at the annual Football Banquet. It was something that I was very proud of, considering we finished with a record of 2-9 and I had just transferred from another University less than five months ago. The presence of the Lord was with me, and I felt like things were going according to His plan. I had developed myself into a leader for the football team and was positioning myself to start finding out about the salvation of the players I shared the field with.

That season showed me that I was being acknowledged as a legitimate threat at the middle linebacker position - an acknowledgement I had worked hard for since high school. The best part about it was that I gave all the glory to God and did not hide it from anyone. At the end of the season, our defensive coordinator left the team and once again, I had another linebacker coach and defensive coordinator. It was not even my fifth year in the college football world and already I had six different position coaches and five different defensive coordinators. The difference this time was that I had someone who shared my passion for the game, and he was a coach who respected his players.

RHODY ROOMMATES NOT EASILY FORGOTTEN

Prior to the start of my first season at Rhode Island, plans had to be made for my living arrangements during doubles. There were basically two options that I had for the upcoming fall semester. The first option was to live on campus in a dorm room which did not seem very appealing, considering I was going on my fourth year in college. The second option at the time seemed too good to pass up. Three other football players were looking for another roommate to live with them in a rented out beach house that was not more than a couple blocks from Scarborough beach. Living off campus during the fall and spring semester for full scholarship football players meant that a generous stipend of approximately $1,600 would be given to each off campus player per semester for rent, utilities and food.

After getting the opportunity to see the beach house, I decided to take the players up on their offer. Our beach house was so close to the ocean you could hear the waves crashing on the shore from the two-story deck on the back of the house. We were about a 20-minute drive from campus, so once I got to the University, I pretty much stayed there the whole day for classes and football practice. Little did I know what I would be confronted with at the beach house that fall semester.

If there was a contest for who could pick the worst roommates that semester, I am pretty sure that I would have been awarded first place three times. There seemed to be little harm living with three football players, but what did I know? The fact was that I was living with a compulsive gambler, who would constantly borrow money from his friends, a compulsive stealer, who would steal from everyone but his roommates, and a chronic marijuana smoker, who frequently invited players and friends over to smoke pot in the basement of the beach house. This was not exactly the kind of environment a Christian would like to find himself living in during college.

How can you take a situation like this and find the positive? The answer is quite simple when you look at it through the eyes of Jesus. I had been given the opportunity to witness to these three players not only through my words but also through my actions. It reminded me of the story in the New Testament when Jesus was sitting down at a table in a house with His disciples, Matthew the Tax Collector and many other tax collectors and sinners. In Matthew 9:11 it says, "And when the Pharisees saw it, they said to His disciples, "Why does your Teacher eat with tax collectors and sinners?". Now Jesus had heard what they said to the disciples and He was more than prepared to answer their question for them. Jesus says to the Pharisees in Matthew 9:12-13, "Those who are well have no need of a physician, but those who are sick. But go and learn what this means: 'I desire mercy and not sacrifice.' For I did not come to call the righteous, but sinners, to repentance."

The Lord blessed me with a golden opportunity to witness to players who did not know Christ. Was it easy when they were throwing parties at the beach house with six kegs of beer, fights breaking out and cops having to come over to break up the parties, due to the neighbors complaining? Of course, not. I was surrounded by temptation at every turn, but the most important thing was that I had Jesus on my side. I knew that Jesus would not give me more than I could handle, although at times, I felt overwhelmed by my living arrangements. Regardless of the environment you find yourself in, you have to take a stand for what you believe in. Don't sell out and give in to peer pressure just because everyone else is doing it. If you can pass that test, that is when you start molding yourself into a leader, instead of just another follower.

There are two things severely affected by peer pressure that I am extremely proud to have avoided in college. The first is that I have never been intoxicated and the second is that I have never been in a fight. That is kind of an oxymoron thing to say when it is coming from a football player. Many people would think the opposite, and many football players live up to that public image to give them reason to believe it is true. When you go against the norm, you start to really surprise yourself and find what you are made of.

That fall semester at the beach house was a time that I learned a great deal about myself. There were quite a few times that I had to say "No" and there were other times that I felt like I was connecting on a spiritual level with my roommates. They respected my belief in Christ and that semester I tried to be a shining light full of optimism amid a disappointing football season. The most memorable moment that semester was not on the football field but in my bedroom at the beach house. It was there that I led our defensive end to come to know the Lord in a personal relationship. Answering God's call was fulfilling me in ways that I thought were not possible. I just wanted to make the most of every opportunity He gave me.

After the fall semester, it was time to say goodbye to those three roommates. I made the decision to move on campus into a dorm room for the spring semester. We learned a lot about each other living in that beach house. The most important lesson I learned is that God can use us in any situation to spread the news about His Son, Jesus Christ. You just have to keep your eyes open and be willing to meet Him halfway.

CHAPTER SEVEN

YOU'RE ONLY AS GOOD AS YOU THINK YOU ARE

Delight yourself also in the Lord, And He shall give you the desires of your heart.
- PSALM 37:4

If you do not get what you want, it is a sure sign that you did not seriously want it.
- RUDYARD KIPLING

I have never in my life envied a human being who led an easy life; I have envied a great many people who led difficult lives and led them well.
- TEDDY ROOSEVELT

WALKING ON HIGHER GROUND AND AWAKENING THE SPIRIT WITHIN

It has been said that the game of football is 90% mental and 10% physical. That is quite a bold statement to make, considering that there is not a play that goes by on the football field without opposing players hitting each other. The truth of the matter is that football is much more than guys just running around and banging helmets. You have to be focused, determined, prepared and mentally alert when taking the football field. These characteristics are what make football the great game it is today. Sure there are plenty of athletes we watch play on Saturday and Sunday who seem born with more talent than they know what to do with on the field. What many do not know is that these same players had to practice to get where they are today. It took preparation and persistence to be successful in their sport. A coach once told me I should aim to get 1% better every practice. It might not seem like a lot but the point is that you are improving everyday at your position. If you're not improving, you're losing ground on achieving your potential.

As each year passes in college, Christian student athletes have the opportunity to mature, not only as players on the field but also as students in the classroom. Just like it is a personal decision whether or not to receive Christ as your personal Savior, it is also your decision whether or not to commit yourself to scholastics and athletics. If the commitment is made to do the best of your ability, you are well on your way to becoming successful in college. It has been said that "when you fail to prepare for something you are preparing to fail." Regardless of your decision in college, you are still in the process of preparing for something good or bad.

As you develop your potential in your sport, many student athletes receive encouragement from family, coaches, peers and friends in high school or college. It always helps to have a solid supporting cast that is behind you. The problem with just having encouragement is that it will only take you so far. You have to truly believe in yourself and have an unshakeable confidence in your abilities. Any room left for doubt will most likely lead to eventual failure in the classroom and on the field. That is why having Christ in your life is so monumental concerning scholastics and athletics, among other countless reasons. Jesus is your strength and confidence, and through Him you can achieve the potential that He has planned for you.

There are going to be some goals in college we set that are not achieved if you aim for the stars. The goals I chose regarding scholastics and athletics were the best case scenario. I'll be the first to admit that I did not achieve them all, but it was not without giving it everything I had. You see, it is not the unfulfilled dreams in college that will discourage you; it is looking back on your college experience and knowing that you had more to give, but were not willing to go the extra mile. After college is over, it is not possible to go back in time. Some people do go back in their minds and play the "should of would of game" in their heads that goes around and around in circles of regret. During my college experience I can honestly say that I gave it everything I had, and I give Jesus all the glory and honor for inspiring me and filling me with the Holy Spirit. By meeting God halfway, He took care of all the other details. Let me help prepare you to reach your God-given potential.

1ST AND 10 IN THE CLASSROOM

Good habits in life do not come naturally. They have to be worked on day in and day out to establish a pattern of consistency that eventually becomes a daily part of your lifestyle. Success on the playing field largely depends on your success in the classroom. Let's face it, if you are not making the grades in high school or college, you might fall below eligibility and not even get to step onto the field. Even if you are just doing enough to get by, you still need the intelligence to understand how the offensive or defensive schemes work to effectively play your position.

Every student athlete needs to develop a game plan on how to prepare to excel in the classroom. The creation of positive repetitive habits in the classroom are essential for getting good grades and making the most of your education. These habits need to be created as early as possible in your education so that they become as routine as brushing your teeth every morning. Early in my education, I followed a simple strategy in the classroom that was utilized throughout college. I like to call it "1st and 10 in the Classroom." It is so simple and straight forward that everyone should be able to follow it. As a matter of fact, there isn't anything I am going to say that you haven't already heard. The only requirement for being able to follow this game plan is that you have to put your good friend, Mr. Lazy, in the closet and not let him out.

All of us are prone to feeling lazy at times. The demands on a student athlete in high school and college are extremely fast paced. There doesn't seem to be a single second to spare. For some student athletes, it always seems that if they are going to slack off, it is in the classroom, rather than in their sport. For some reason, the classroom takes a back seat to sports. You would think it would be the other way around considering we are going to be utilizing our education in the working world for the rest of our life. Our accomplishments on the field are fulfilling but will ultimately lead to short-lived memories and uncomfortable bodily injuries that never heal quite right.

The 1st and 10 in the classroom approach I took consisted of five different steps to be successful. The key to this approach is that you never give yourself the chance to get behind in your classes. Just like on the football field when you have a fresh set of downs on the offense, you can always be 1st and 10 in the classroom if you follow these steps. The first step consists of never missing any of your classes due to laziness. This is obviously the hardest step because in college, there are countless reasons you can come up with to miss a class when you're tired. The problem is that the majority of these reasons are a result of being lazy. If you miss a class, you are allowing yourself to get behind and are already increasing your chances of failure in the classroom. During my five years of college, I missed a total of less than three classes. My body was paying a price for my education due to football, and I wanted to learn as much as possible.

The second step to always having a fresh set of downs in the classroom is to sit in the front of the class. This helps you to pay better attention to what the teacher is communicating, reduces your chances of falling asleep, gives you a better opportunity to get involved in class discussions, and you become a familiar face to your teacher. During my college education, there were countless teachers that I became good friends with as a result of sitting in the front of the class and participating in classroom discussions. A professional student/teacher relationship with one of my Finance professors resulted in receiving the PACAP/CBA Scholarship: Excellence in Finance at the University of Rhode Island in 1997 and 1998 due to his high recommendation of my accomplishments in scholastics and athletics.

The third step is to take notes while you are attending your classes. When you actively write down what the teacher is saying, there is a better chance that you will retain the information that is being taught. These notes really come in handy when studying for your tests, because good teachers go out of the way to tell you the course material to study. I can remember football players who would skip classes and ask other student athletes to take their notes for them. When you do something like that, you are just cheating yourself and not making the most of your education.

The fourth step is crucial to success in the classroom. You should complete all homework assignments, papers and projects that are assigned by your teacher. Not only does completing this work help with your grade in the class, but it gives you practice preparing yourself for what you will be tested on. Without completing coursework assigned by the teacher, you are decreasing your chances of being successful in your class and instead of being 1st and 10 you become more like 4th and 7.

The last step should be common sense, but you might be surprised how many student athletes do not bother doing it. It is essential that you study for all upcoming tests. The real key to this final step, due to tests usually being worth a good portion of your grade, is that you start studying a couple days prior to your test and not just the night before. Some student athletes think that by cramming it in the night before they will remember everything. The truth is that some classes just have too much information to prepare this way and retention of the material will be greater if it is done over several days.

Everyone has the ability to follow these five steps to being successful in the classroom. There is no hiding that it is going to require a great deal of work. The only thing that can hold you back is being lazy. It is so easy to do when no one is looking over your shoulder. This is an opportunity to be responsible for your actions and mature into an adult. I have always viewed completing these steps as short term sacrifice for long term benefits and rewards. The more time you invest in scholastics now, the greater you will be rewarded in your future employment. I encourage you to give it your best shot. When you achieve success in the classroom and give all the glory to God, that is when you start creating your own luck out of good old fashioned hard work. You just might be surprised at the opportunities that come your way.

WALKING ON HIGHER GROUND AND AWAKENING THE SPIRIT WITHIN

SCHOOL'S FINALLY OUT FOR THE SUMMER

The end of another year of college came to a close after the spring semester and the completion of spring ball in 1998. The difference this time was that I was at another college, and my situation could not have been any better. I finally had a position coach/defensive coordinator, by the name of Coach Narduzzi, who was willing to instruct me on the field and in the film room to help me achieve my potential at middle linebacker. It was the first spring ball I had participated in college as the 1st string middle linebacker. The upcoming season at URI would mark my last year of college football as a 5th year super senior, and I was looking for it to be my breakout season.

After spending the past three summers in summer school at the University of Kentucky, I decided to head home to Cleveland for the summer after completing my first full year at the University of Rhode Island. The strength and conditioning program that needed to be followed during the summer was something I felt could be completed on my own. The conditioning test I had to prepare for consisted of enough sprints to make up a mile around a track while the lifting exercises were built toward achieving my highest three rep max on bench, power clean and squat.

At the end of my spring semester, I said goodbye to my teammates and friends for the summer and packed up my 1992 Ford Tempo to head to Cleveland at 10:00 o'clock at night. The drive was a solid 10 plus hours so I liked to drive through the night to avoid any traffic. I can still remember crossing over the George Washington Bridge in New York around 2:00 a.m. and hitting a huge pothole that made my head hit the roof of the car as the pots and pans rattled in the backseat. Needless to say, I was more than awake after that for the remainder of the trip.

My plans that summer consisted of basically three things. Prior to driving to Cleveland for the summer, I updated my resume because I was very interested in finding a paying internship in a finance related position. My previous work experience consisted of an internship with an insurance company in Lexington, KY, self-employment as a certified personal trainer, and working with my father at a steel coil company in Maple Heights, OH. I liked to call it an internship in operations management, which was a very fancy way of saying that I banded coils with metal straps eight hours a day after they were treated in acid and coated with a protective coating. The use of the words, "operations management," could be slightly construed as a strong play of words, but you would be surprised how I could justify it by talking about the operations at the facility.

The other two things I wanted to accomplish were making a trip to Lexington, KY for about a week to visit my good friend, Big Mike, and sticking to the strength and conditioning program for the duration of the summer. I was really looking forward to not having to take any classes for the first time in three years. Instead I was hoping to land a good paying internship that would give me solid work experience in finance. The future looked bright, but in case football at the next level did not work out, I wanted to build a solid resume in college to make myself marketable in Corporate America after graduation.

After getting settled at my parent's house, it wasn't long before I was back on the road and heading to Lexington. I was excited to see some old friends and tell them how the new college was treating me. It is amazing how the Lord can call you into action even when you are on vacation. After a couple days in Lexington with Big Mike, I found myself in a restaurant with one of the offensive lineman for the Wildcats. He was a good friend during my time at Kentucky and that night we talked about him receiving the Lord in his life. He told me that he wasn't ready to make that kind of commitment, and that he had plenty of time to settle down. For some reason, I felt like I needed to break through the pride and stubbornness, but that was not God's plan that night. All I could do was plant the seed of faith and hope that the Lord would water it.

That night proved to be a valuable lesson in that when we try to reach people for Christ, everyone is at different stages in their lives. I believe the Lord uses us to cultivate the weary and unsaved in different ways. Some of us might plow the heart of someone who has never heard the word of God. Others could pick out the rocks and sticks that are holding that person back in their life. Another person could come along and plant the seed, and the ultimate gardener is Jesus, as He waters the seed and allows it to grow into a believer.

Did you know that every time an unbeliever comes to know their personal Savior, Jesus Christ, there is rejoicing in heaven by the angels? Another soul has just been added to the kingdom of God for eternity. It is an awesome blessing to be part of this process. Jesus loves us so much that He blesses us with individual talents and allows us to utilize them in our lives to fulfill His purpose for us. We are called to give Him all the glory and honor in our lives.

That time in the restaurant in Lexington would be the last time I would ever see that Wildcat offensive lineman. You see, he thought that he had all the time in the world to make a personal decision to receive Christ. I wonder how many of you reading this book feel that way. You're young, bright and have the whole world in front of you. That is how my friend felt when I was talking to him. Little did he know that when he went to Ohio State for a weekend trip, a car would slam into his 280 pound plus frame in downtown Columbus, and a few days later, he would die in the hospital at 22 years old. I don't know if my friend ever received Jesus in his heart, but I'm grateful that I can look back and remember talking to him about my personal Savior.

On my trip back to Cleveland, I had to prepare myself for an interview with the Vice-President of the Treasury Department at the Sherwin-Williams Company in downtown Cleveland. I have to give the credit to my mom for making this possible. She met the Vice-President of Treasury where she worked, and through small talk, shared that her son was finishing his degree in Finance and was looking for a summer internship. That is where the interview came into the picture. After I called the number on the business card that the Vice President provided, she was impressed with what she heard on the phone. She was eager to schedule an appointment for me to come in for an interview at my earliest convenience. The following week, I drove to the Sherwin-Williams Corporate Headquarters for the interview. Before I knew it, I was hired by Sherwin-Williams as an intern to work 40 hours a week during the summer at $12 dollars an hour. Pulling in $480 a week was great money for a summer job, and more importantly, I was learning about what I wanted to pursue after college, and adding experience to my resume in the process.

That summer flew by, as I was working at Sherwin-Williams and preparing for the upcoming football season in the weight room and on the track. I weighed about 225 lbs and was hoping to keep my weight steady with preparation for the run test when I reported back to Rhode Island. It was nice to be home and getting to spend some quality time with my parents and brother during the summer. It was hard being over 10 hours away from home at college, but they supported me, because they knew how hard I worked to start in college games as a middle linebacker. The previous season they didn't miss a single home game which is quite an accomplishment. The drive to and from Rhode Island and Cleveland was over 20 hours. Some home games were back-to-back, and even though we finished 2-9 my first season, my family was just happy to see me back on the field, making tackles again. Support like that is hard to come by, and I consider myself truly blessed to have such a great family there for me during college and far beyond.

SYMBOLISM OF THE NUMBER 40

The summer was coming to a close and the start of my last college football season was quickly approaching. This season I would be wearing the number 40 that followed me through high school to the University of Kentucky before having to sit out a season at the University of Rhode Island. This number went far beyond just being an identity for me on the football field. It was symbolic of my relationship with my personal Savior and Lord, Jesus Christ, because it is one of the most significant and important numbers used throughout the Old and New Testament. The fact that I had the opportunity to display that number on the field as I played my senior year was a privilege and an honor.

Many people are familiar with the story of Noah building the ark in Genesis before it proceeded to rain for 40 days and 40 nights which flooded the entire earth. Only Noah, his family and the animals on the ark were spared to multiply and continue life on earth. It would be the first and last time God would allow such drastic devastation. His promise to us from that day on has been the rainbow you see in the sky after it rains. Something so beautiful that only the very hands of God could have created it.

If we fast forward to the New Testament there is another familiar passage in Matthew that talks about how Jesus fasted for forty days and forty nights in the wilderness. It was during this time that Jesus was tempted by Satan. Every time the devil tried to get Jesus to do something that would prove to be a sin, Jesus would quote Scripture from memory.

After the third time Satan tried to tempt Jesus, He simply replied in Matthew 4:10, "Away with you, Satan! For it is written, You shall worship the Lord your God, and Him only you shall serve." If the Son of God was not exempt from being tempted by Satan, how much more does that make us vulnerable to the devil's deceit and lies? The protection for that vulnerability can be found in 2 Timothy 3:16 where it says, "All Scripture is given by inspiration of God, and is profitable for doctrine, for reproof, for correction, for instruction in righteousness, that the man of God may be complete, thoroughly equipped for every good work." Jesus answered Satan with nothing but the very inspired words of God and understood that nothing could be more powerful or encompassing against sin and temptation.

Those are two very familiar passages that reference the number 40 but I want to go above and beyond those two times to show the significance of this special number. In Exodus 16:35 it says, "And the children of Israel ate manna forty years, until they came to an inhabited land; they ate manna until they came to the border of the land of Canaan." This proved to be so significant because God was providing for his people in the wilderness after the Israelites crossed the Red Sea with Moses. Although the Lord freed His people from bondage from the Egyptians, if it wasn't for His provision in the wilderness they would not have survived.

The Israelites were not without complaint as they ate manna for forty years and Moses would talk to God alone to ask for direction and forgiveness for the Israelites sins. In Exodus 24:18 it says, "So Moses went into the midst of the cloud and went up into the mountain. And Moses was on the mountain forty days and forty nights." It was during this time that God provided Moses with the instructions to build the Ark for the Testimony. Later in Exodus 34:28 Moses again visited with the Lord, "So he was there with the Lord forty days and forty nights; he neither ate bread nor drank water. And He wrote on the tablets the words of the covenant, the Ten Commandments."

As the Israelites continued on their journey in the wilderness to the promise land, the Lord wanted them to spy on the people of Canaan before He would give them victory. Numbers 13:25 says, "And they returned from spying out the land after forty days." After all the countless miracles the Lord performed for the Israelites, the people still didn't think that their God could deliver the enemies of Canaan into their hands. Due to their refusal to enter Canaan from a total lack of faith, the Lord passed a harsh judgment on His people. The judgment was in Numbers 14:33-34 that says, "And your sons shall be shepherds in the wilderness forty years, and bear the brunt of your infidelity, until your carcasses are consumed in the wilderness. According to the number of the days in which you spied out the land, forty days, for each day you shall bear your guilt one year, namely forty years, and you shall know my rejection."

The story of David defeating Goliath prior to becoming King of Israel is one of the best stories of bravery every told. Prior to David killing Goliath, 1 Samuel 17:16 says, "And the Phillistine drew near and presented himself forty days, morning and evening." That's right! It took forty days of Goliath ridiculing the Israelites before David took a bold leap of faith and had the Lord deliver the giant into his hands. It can also be found in the Old Testament that King Saul, David and Solomon each reigned for 40 years.

The last reference I will use to the number 40 being used in the Bible is what I believe is truly the greatest. Our eternal salvation would not be possible if Jesus, the Son of God, did not die for our sins. The one infallible thing that secures Jesus as truly being the Son of God is that He conquered death by rising from the grave after three days. In Acts 1:3 the proof is delivered when it is said, "To whom He also presented Himself alive after His suffering by many infallible proofs, being seen by them during forty days and speaking of the things pertaining to the kingdom of God." After Jesus died on the cross for our sins, He not only rose from the grave but appeared before the disciples and others for a period of forty days before transcending into heaven to sit at the right hand of the Father.

The number 40 for some might just be two random numbers put together on a football jersey, but to me it was so much more. This special number paved the way for the creation of the mystical rainbow. It helped me understand how to overcome temptation while enabling me to become intimately familiar with the provisions of the Lord and His very Commandments. Number 40 helped me to take a bold leap of faith like David, and most importantly, it showed me that Jesus is the very Son of God. When you look at the number 40 after reading this I hope it takes on a special meaning for you as it does for me. As I prepared myself for my final college football season, the number 40 was ready to give Jesus all the glory and honor regardless of the outcome my senior season. As long as I met Him halfway, I knew He would provide according to His will for my life.

FIFTH YEAR SENIOR SEASON DEDICATED TO MY DAD

I have always respected and appreciated my dad and the sacrifices he has made for our family. Besides having big biceps and a passion for working out, my father has always been an extremely hard worker. For as long as I could remember, my dad has worked the night shift, and usually, he would register up to 10 to 12 hours per night after overtime. There were no interior motives to working those long hours day in and day out throughout my childhood besides providing the best he could for his family. When we moved to the country in Medina, OH, my dad commuted back and forth to work almost an hour each way, so my brother and I could go to the same school. If it wasn't for his commitment to his family along with my mother's love and encouragement, I can honestly say that I would not be where I am today.

When I reached my last year of college football, I wanted to do something special for my dad to show how much I loved him and appreciated his dedication to his family. It is rapidly becoming a rarity in this country to find fathers that provide for their families. The number of children growing up without their paternal fathers is alarming due to the high divorce rate and children born to single mothers out-of-wedlock. I decided to write my father a card that told him that I wanted to dedicate my senior season to him. I know it wasn't much but I wanted him to know that as I made tackles on that grassy field, it was through his hard work that being at Rhode Island was even possible. I wanted him to be able to live the college football experience through me.

My dad wasn't raised with just one younger brother like myself and given the chance to truly enjoy his childhood years. Instead he lived in a house with two brothers and four sisters. I remember hearing stories about how his mother would bring a watermelon home from the store and if you didn't act fast there would be nothing left. In his teenage years my dad lost one of his sisters to an illness that took her life, and from a young age, he was working to help support the family. My father did not have the luxury of just being a kid and focusing on school and sports. I believe to this day that if my father had grown up in my circumstances and had the support and encouragement I had, he would not only have played college football, but would have played at the next level. I owed my senior season to him, and I was going to make it one to remember.

RHODY DEFENSE MAKES A STATEMENT

From the very beginning of doubles my senior year, everyone on the defensive side of the ball knew that we had the making of a special defense. Our star defensive end who was sidelined a year ago with a broken leg was back in the starting lineup. The linebacker unit was stronger and more experienced than the previous season, while the secondary was pretty solid with many returning starters. Practices during doubles were dominated by the first team defense, which was encouraging on our side, but raised questions about the validity of our offense. .

A good defense will only take a team so far if the offense isn't capable of producing many points. My fear was that as the season started our offense would not be able to put up at least 21 points per game. I remember one practice during doubles when the offensive line coach made a statement about the tenacity of the linebackers. Our new defensive coordinator/linebacker coach was adamant about his linebackers attacking downhill at the snap of the ball. That was exactly what we did during practice and it was paying big dividends when it came time to watch practice film. The offensive line coach was frustrated because of the fact that his linemen couldn't get a block on any of the linebackers attacking downhill. Every play that was keyed as a run would have to contend with three blitzing linebackers who were looking to fill their gap and hit someone in a hurry.

After two weeks of doubles it was time to get my senior season started. Our first game was against William & Mary at our home field, and it would speak volumes of how the rest of the season would unfold. The game started with our starting quarterback suffering a partially separated left shoulder on the offenses first possession. The second string quarterback was a true freshman, and in his defense, a lack of college experience can haunt a quarterback on the ever-present dangerous football field, especially when you don't have much time in the pocket to pass. Although our defense came out to play that day, we gave up three scoring drives that resulted in touchdowns which proved to be too much to overcome as we lost the first game of the season 13-21.

TAKING ON A LEADERSHIP ROLE

There comes a time in a student athlete's life where he has the opportunity to take a leadership role. What that entails is not only being accountable for your actions on the field but also serving as an example for others to follow. You need to be someone others can count on when things get tough and the path is treacherous - someone who is willing to motivate and encourage other fellow teammates, even when the forecast is dark and cloudy with a 90% chance of rain. It is a big role to fill, but if you step up to the plate, you'll be a better player for it and learn a valuable life lesson in the process.

That is the ground that I stood on as we headed into the second game of the season against the Richmond Spiders. I had never been one to lead others through loud words, but rather preferred to lead through example of my actions on the football field. The fact was that we were already 0-1, and I felt that being vocal about the immediate future of this football team was something that needed to be communicated to the players. We needed to practice like we were going to win and envision ourselves doing just that on Saturday. I couldn't let the season just go by without knowing that I did everything I could for us to be successful.

There are a lot of good leaders in this world that we live in, but great leaders are hard to come by. I knew that being a good leader would not satisfy me, because in reality being good is just doing enough to being better than average. It means you are working hard, but not as hard as you know you can work to be great. Giving it everything you have is what I wanted. Having no regrets looking back was what I envisioned for myself regardless of the outcome on the field. Being a great leader is stated best by Teddy Roosevelt when he said,

It is not the critic who counts: not the man who points out how the strong man stumbles or where the doer of deeds could have done better. The credit belongs to the man who is actually in the arena, whose face is marred by dust and sweat and blood, who strives valiantly, who errs and comes up short again and again, because there is no effort without error or shortcoming, but who knows the great enthusiasms, the great devotions, who spends himself for a worthy cause; who, at the best, knows, in the end, the triumph of high achievement, and who, at the worst, if he fails, at least he fails while daring greatly, so that his place shall never be with those cold and timid souls who knew neither victory nor defeat."

That is what it means to me to be a great leader - going above and beyond the call of duty because of the passion that burns inside on you. I encourage you to try to be the person that Teddy Roosevelt describes in the passage above. Whether you succeed or fail, you will be doing it with all your heart, and in the very end, I can promise you will amazed at how lucky you get in life. The reason luck will come your way is because the secret of getting "lucky" in life is working hard and giving God all the glory and honor. Luck should really be referred to as a blessing from God because the Creator of the Universe knows and helps guide us along our path in life by opening doors and closing others at His appointed time.

As the second game of the season quickly approached, I suddenly found myself being a true leader on the practice field. If we were going to win against Richmond it had to start with a change of attitude and effort on the practice field. I made a point of being more vocal in the huddles and positively encouraged the defensive players every chance I got. It was also important to continue to focus on getting better every practice and being open to constructive criticism from the coaches. After all, it is through coaching that we continue to develop our potential at our positions. After what I thought was a great week of practice, the team was prepared and excited for the Richmond Spiders to come to town.

PLAYING IN THE ZONE

There comes a special time in every athlete's career where he has an experience in a sport that supersedes what was thought possible in the realm of play. That place is commonly referred to in athletics as "playing in the zone." That is exactly where I ventured when the Richmond Spiders came to Meade Stadium. This game would be the highlight of my college football career and push me to my outermost limits as a player. It would also prove to be another time that the game of football taught me valuable lessons about life.

This was definitely a special day for me. During the week leading up to the Richmond game, I was chosen to be one of the three team captains. Early that morning before the game, the coaching staff let me lead the chapel service for the players who wanted to attend. The Lord was using me to spread His word to the University of Rhode Island football players, and I considered it an honor and privilege. To top it off, the program guide for the game had none other than a picture of me against Brown on the front cover.

As I suited up for the game that day, I went through my usual pre-game routine. I modestly put on my shirt that said "I will not be denied" as a reminder of what I had been through to get to this point in my career. As I taped my wrists, I wrote Philippians 4:13 on one wrist and on the other wrist I wrote "The Lord is with me; I fear nothing." I always had the same head trainer tape my ankles before every game because that was also part of the routine. I'm happy to say that I had never been one of those players who do not wash their jock strap, socks or undershirt for the entire season, using them as a good luck charm. I always thought that was a little on the gross side.

Prior to the game, I could feel a razor sharp focus coming on that I had not experienced before. As the game started, there was certainly an unyielding spirit that was not willing to accept failure for my actions on the field. I believe it was the very Holy Spirit of God who helped take me to a level of play that I had never experienced. The Holy Spirit consumed me as I took charge of the defense that day.

During the course of our game against the Richmond Spiders, it literally felt like I was involved in every play. Regardless of who came out to block me, my opponents were merely a momentary obstacle to overcome to get to the ball carrier or quarterback. As the tackles I made that day mounted, the natural course of the game was heading for overtime. It wouldn't take just one overtime to decide the winner of this colossal match up of stingy defenses; it would take three.

A crucial point in the game came for me when we were in the third overtime. My body was physically exhausted from running from sideline to sideline. I remember making a tackle and being so exhausted that I wasn't sure that I could get up off the ground. My body was extremely overheated as I was gasping for breath to replenish my oxygen deprived and burning lungs. At that moment, I talked to Jesus on the football field for a momentary second. I simply said, "Jesus, if this is what it takes to be a great player then I don't want it." After five years of college football, I came to a point in my career where I couldn't push myself any further. It felt as if I reached my limit, and I now understood what it would take to be a great player, but my body didn't want any part of it. Suddenly a peace came over me, and it felt as if Jesus was saying, "Don't worry, I'll get you through this. Trust me. I never said it would be easy but it will be worth it". At that second, I got back up and kept playing with everything I had for the remainder of the game.

I wish I could say that this awakening led to us winning our second game of the season in triple overtime but that wasn't the case. The Richmond Spiders scored a touchdown in the third overtime while our offense only kicked a field goal. It was a devastating 14-20 loss for the team after a hard-fought battle, but someone had to lose. Although I was disappointed with the loss, I was pleased that every drop of sweat, ounce of energy and bit of strength were left on that field. I held nothing back that day as I registered a URI single game record of 19 tackles.

After the game, I spent the afternoon with my parents and brother. We enjoyed the day together as we watched football, talked and ate at my favorite restaurant called the China Buffet. It was nice to get my mind off football, but once they departed back to Cleveland for the long 10 hour drive on Saturday night, I couldn't help but think about the game. The next morning I drove to Narragansett Beach and walked barefoot on the beach, thinking about how a great deal of energy and time were wasted for another loss or was it? If I gave it everything I had, what was there to be ashamed of in a defeat? The team might have lost, but I viewed it as a victory for myself, due to not giving up on the field, even when my body and mind were certainly not on the same page as my unyielding spirit. We failed as a team that day, but I realized that failure is inevitable in life if you want to be successful. The important thing is to continue to dare greatly in your pursuits, and you'll eventually be able to taste the ripened fruits of victory. God wants to bless us; we just have to keep fighting and believing in ourselves.

The URI Rams had started the 1998 football season at 0-2. Two close games decided by 7 points or less was all that separated us from being undefeated. As we went to the football meeting on Monday afternoon, it was announced to the team that I was chosen as Defensive Player of the Week in the Atlantic 10 Conference for my 19 tackle performance in the triple overtime loss to the Richmond Spiders. It was a shock and an honor to be recognized for my performance in a game that we lost in triple overtime. I certainly gave Jesus all the glory for this accomplishment, because without Him, it would not have been possible. This recognition further convinced me that I could only be limited on the field by the boundaries I had set up in my mind. If I could tear down those boundaries and truly trust Jesus, then His will would dictate my potential.

BEING AN AUTHENTIC AND GENUINE ROLE MODEL

There seems to be a misconception about exactly whom student athletes are role models to in our generation. Some people think that this only applies to the fans that are watching in the stands. What about the younger players who are waiting for their turn to shine on the field? It makes sense to me that being an authentic and genuine role model to them is just as important (if not more important) than to the fans in the stands. After all, it is your younger teammates who are going to eventually influence their fans in either a positive or negative manner. If we can reach out to them and show them how important it is to play with Christ in their lives and walk on higher ground, how much more will that be able to affect the younger generation?

On countless occasions in the locker room, I have seen players who might say one thing but do something completely different. I remember at the University of Rhode Island a number of players who smoked marijuana and didn't care that it would hurt the team. These same players sat in team meetings and acted as if they were on board with the rules and regulations of the team. That wasn't sending a very good message to the younger players right out of high school. It would be nice if student athletes could say "What you see is what you get." They should not have hidden agendas. They should actually do what they commit themselves to in their lives. If that could be accomplished, it would completely change the way the world views college football athletes.

I remember watching the Indiana Pacers and Detroit Pistons playing basketball on television over a year ago. The reason the game was so memorable is because of what happened at the end. There was a hard foul by the Pacers, which resulted in a harder push from one of the Pistons. This, of course, escalated to multiple players getting ejected from the game. As one of the Indiana Pacers was lying on a table by the team bench, a Detroit fan threw a cup of water from the stands onto the player. Instead of ignoring what happened, the player decided to go into the stands to find and hit the fan who threw the cup of water. This did not go over well with the fans and before you knew it, there was a brawl between players and fans. It was hard to believe, and at the same time, I could not help but to think of what kind of message this was sending to our younger generation. The player for the Pacers had a decision to make. He could have walked on higher ground and ignored what had happened, but instead, he let his emotions get the best of him. It was an act of selfishness without thinking about what type of ramifications there would be.

When it comes to acting as first class role models in our society, it seems like many athletes are satisfied flying coach or worse yet, even waiting for a standby ticket. From allegations of steroid use in Major League Baseball, and Track and Field, to unruly behavior on the basketball court, players are not taking their job as role models seriously. Athletes are blessed to be where they are today, and instead of helping influence the younger generation in a positive way, they continue to fall short. I know we were born into sin and that the only perfect person is the Son of God. However, when you are in a position to influence others, you have to find a way to rise above the muck and mud that tries to negatively influence you. My question for you is: Are you willing to take a stand for what is right by helping your teammates and positively influencing your fans?

As the third game of my senior season neared, I wanted to be focused on winning our first game against Northeastern, and also to positively influence our younger players. I wanted to mentor them in the game of football and encourage them to take advantage of their education. Challenging them to walk the straight and narrow through a relationship with Jesus Christ while pursuing their dreams could make all the difference in their lives.

STRIVING FOR THE TACKLE RECORD

Our team traveled to Northeastern for yet another loss, due to failure to score enough points and too many turnovers. We were 0-3, and our next opponent was the Brown Bears, for the coveted Governor's Cup. This time, the Rams would earn their first victory of the season by winning 44-16. As each week passed during my senior season, I wrote a journal of my performance on the field and thoughts for improvement. After recently reading what I had written so many years ago, one thing was evident. Whether or not we won or lost our game, I was never satisfied with how I played. I always thought about the plays I could have made instead of focusing on the plays that were made. A trap that a good deal of players fall into is thinking too much about the game film that has to be watched during practice. What you should be doing is taking one play at a time and learning from the previous play, but not dwelling on it. You need to focus on the play at hand and envision yourself being successful. Most of all, you should enjoy being out there playing college football.

The second victory of the season came against the Maine Bears, with a last second field goal that propelled us to an 18-17 victory. This was the only game of the season where I had to voluntarily leave the game. It happened in the fourth quarter when one of my players smashed into the side of my helmet. Something did not feel right so I went to the sidelines. The head trainer asked me my name, what day it was and what I had for breakfast. After successfully answering those three questions, I told him that I could not help but to think of the board game Candy Land and that for some crazy reason, it frightened me. That was enough proof for him to diagnose me with a mild concussion, and I sat out the remaining minutes of the fourth quarter as our team went on to win.

Week in and week out, I played with all my heart and tried to motivate the team. Even though our record was not where I would have liked it to be, I focused on the positive aspects of the season. I was leading the conference in tackles for the second season in a row and on pace to break the single season record at URI of 151 tackles. Our defense was ranked second in the conference for total defense behind the Richmond Spiders. I also achieved something that very few players get to experience in college football or the pros. The media had established a nickname for me. Some of the greatest football nicknames of all time that I can remember are "Broadway" Joe, "Mean" Joe Greene, "The Blonde Bomber" and Elroy "Crazy Legs" Hirsch. When number 40 made a tackle on the field, the announcer wouldn't say "Viera" but rather "The Hitman" on the tackle. That's right, number 40 was known as Miguel "The Hitman" Viera in the college football world.

My last senior home game of the season was against the UMASS Minutemen, who were the #1 ranked Division I AA team in the country. They coincidentally went on that year to win the National Championship. Family day was scheduled during this game, and prior to the opening kickoff, parents of the seniors were introduced to the crowd. It was an emotional time, getting to see my parents out there on the field. They were so very supportive during my football career (along with my brother), and it meant a lot to me to get to share this special moment with them. For the past two years, they had driven to every home game and probably racked up enough miles on the van to drive across the country and back.

The UMASS game was a hard fought battle, but eventually we lost, due to a lack of offense. The real story behind this game was what happened with :50 seconds remaining on the clock. The Minutemen were running out the clock, and the quarterback was getting set to take a knee. As their center (who was obviously nursing a bad leg) snapped the ball, I ran him over like a freight train en route to the quarterback who took a knee directly behind the center. This created a lot of tension with the other team, and the referee ejected me from the game for simply playing too hard. Later that week, I read in the paper that I was ejected from the game for supposedly spitting in the opponent's face. That just goes to show you how the media likes to spice up a story for the paper!

Our last game of the season was against Brian Westbrook and the Villanova Wildcats on the road in Philadelphia. Our record for the season was a dismal 3-7 by this time and we had just come off a 7-9 loss to Jerry Azumah and the New Hampshire Wildcats. All the seniors wanted was to finish the season with a victory. All season, I had given it everything I had, but the overall team record looked as if no one was even trying. The Villanova game proved to be no different than the other seven losses that season as our offense only put up 15 points en route to a season ending 15-26 loss. We put forth so much effort, and yet, we won only one more game than the previous season. One thing that I was proud of that season was that I had unofficially registered 155 tackles in 11 games to beat the previous URI single season record of 151 tackles. The reason I say unofficially is because the Atlantic 10 Conference only credited me with 140 tackles my senior season. However, in my heart I knew the real numbers.

After the last game of the season, I took pictures with family, friends and coaches on the field. It was a long journey to reach my final collegiate game, and it felt as if I were literally graduating from college football. I once heard the saying "It is not the journey, but the destination, that matters." I know there is a place for me in heaven when my life on earth comes to an end, but until that day comes, I'm going to enjoy every second of the journey. You have to learn to take the good with the bad in this roller coaster ride we call life. Even though we finished 3-8 that season, I developed friendships that would last a lifetime and got to do the Lord's work through spreading the gospel to teammates and friends. I was chosen as one of four permanent captains for the 1998 season and had earned the respect of my fellow teammates. The question was where would I go from here? It was going to take another step of faith now that college football was finally over.

CHAPTER EIGHT

LIFE BEYOND COLLEGE ATHLETICS

When I was a child, I spoke as a child, I understood as a child, I thought as a child; but when I became a man, I put away childish things.
— 1 CORINTHIANS 13:11

Success is not the key to happiness. Happiness is the key to success. If you love what you are doing you will be successful.
— ALBERT SCHWEITZER

I, the Lord, search the heart, I test the mind, Even to give every man according to his own ways, According to the fruit of his doings.
— JEREMIAH 17:10

*T*his world can become an intimidating place when college comes to an end. That is when what I like to call "the real world" begins. It is the world of grocery shopping, monthly rent, energy consumption bills, medical bills and you name it; you pay it. It can be even more devastating to a full scholarship athlete, because the past four to five years at college included room, board, books and meals at no cost other than some bumps and bruises. Once you graduate from college, whether you like to admit it or not, your life will dramatically change. I'm not implying that it is going to necessarily change for the better or worse, because that is entirely up to you. That depends upon your preparation for your post-college life prior to graduation. Like I said earlier, "failing to prepare is preparing to fail."

Now don't start getting the cold sweats on me if you are graduating in the near future and are still trying to figure out what you want to do with your life. I want your transition to the working world or maybe even professional sports to be as smooth as possible. There are steps you can take to minimize your risk and give you the best opportunity to get a great-paying job out of college. A sound resume, excellent social skills and an optimistic attitude will take you a long way. Don't forget about the most important thing. If you are a Christian, you have Jesus Christ, the very Son of God on your side. He will be there for you to guide and direct your every step if you seek Him with all your heart.

I'm hoping my post-college story can offer some insight and direction into where you want to go from here. We live in the best country in the world, and you can be whatever you put your mind to in life. If you believe in yourself and you feel that God is directing you in a certain way, there is nothing to lose by going for it. You have been put through the demanding schedule of a student athlete for the past four to five years. It is exactly the type of training that helps you succeed in the working world. If you were like me, you became very savvy at managing your time efficiently to complete your education and at the same time, to excel in your collegiate sport. Employers are looking for workers just like you to help their company grow. Get that pen or pencil ready to take some notes, because I'm about to take you on a tour of the post-college world.

ASPIRATIONS FOR THE NEXT LEVEL

Upon the completion on my senior season at URI, there were still a number of questions that I had unanswered regarding football. After playing 11 college games that season and making a truckload of tackles, my body would need several months to heal my hyper-extended elbow, bruised calf muscle, stiff neck and sore lower back. The problem with giving yourself time to heal after the season is that there is not really any time if you want to play at the next level. Once the season is complete, the elite college NFL draft prospects get invited to showcase their talent and work with NFL coaches at games like the East-West Shrine Game, the Hula Bowl and the Senior Bowl.

At the end of the season, the good Lord blessed me with accolades that personified what it meant to be able to make every tackle for Jesus on the field. Even though we won only three games that season, I was named on the First-Team All-Conference Defense for the Atlantic 10 Conference and for the second year in a row, led the A-10 in tackles. In addition, I was named a Second-Team All-American for Division I AA football, recognized as a First-Team Academic All-American, for my grades and was ranked as the 35th best middle linebacker in the country based on the ratings for the 1999 NFL draft.

The most memorable award that year came at the URI Football Banquet when I was named as the team's Most Valuable Player. This is an award that to this day I hold dear to my heart because it was voted for by the players on the team. It was truly an honor and privilege to know that my efforts to lead and encourage my teammates were recognized by the players. Although I did not have a speech prepared as I stood at the podium in front of the players, coaches and parents, I utilized my opportunity to tell them about my personal Savior. I told them that without Jesus in my life, this award would not have been possible. Everyone in that room heard me give the Son of God all the glory and honor that day. I told them that because Jesus shed his blood for me on the cross at Calvary without sin, my sins in the past, present and future have been forgiven. Not only would my sins be separated from me farther than the East is from the West but I would also be given the opportunity to spend eternity in heaven after this life is complete.

Of course, there were some blank stares in the crowd that day, but I was not interested in whether I offended anyone. I simply wanted to share the truth about Jesus Christ. That might sound like a cruel thing to say for some people, but the truth is that without Jesus in your life, you are not going to heaven. That is not something I came up with out of the blue, but it is what the Bible says in John 3:16. Now if you are not going to heaven, then where do you think you'll be going? The only two places people go when they die is either heaven or hell. The sad thing is the number of people that do not realize they are not going to heaven.

It was an emotional speech as I let the Holy Spirit give me the words to say. At one point in the speech, I held up the MVP trophy and told the defense that they were just as deserving of this award. That year our defense finished second in the A-10 conference in total defense, which is quite an accomplishment considering our eight losses. I told the players that it was a shame that our society recognized victory from failure based on the amount of wins or losses you have. There was definitely an untold story that year about the Rhode Island players persevering through the season. They continued to fight and never gave up, which was something that those players should have been proud of that season. A couple of years later, it would be the freshman and sophomore players who would turn the URI football program around. For the first time in a long time, they were ranked as one of the top 25 Division I AA college football teams in the national polls throughout their winning season of 8-3.

The extent of my brush with the NFL after my senior season consisted of a scout from the New England Patriots coming to the University of Rhode Island to test me, one of our offensive linemen, and our transfer running back from Clemson. We each benched 225 pounds for as many reps as we could get and were timed in the shuttle run and the 40-yard dash. I even signed with an agent in Providence, but he didn't materialize any leads for a tryout in the NFL. I wasn't invited to a NFL combine and to be honest with you, there seemed to be absolutely no interest from anyone. It was not very long after the season that I realized that my football career was possibly coming to an end.

HANGING UP THE CLEATS

One of the most difficult things you will ever have to do if you really love the sport you play is to eventually hang up your cleats for good. It is my fear that your experience with playing at the next level will be the same as mine. What I hope is that you make the most of your college education and have a degree in something you enjoy. The great thing about a solid bachelor's degree in college is that you don't have to put all your hopes and dreams in one bucket. If the NFL works out, that is fantastic. If it doesn't, you have a college degree to fall back on. The NFL is really the best of the best. If you want to play in the NFL, you have to be willing to put your body on the line every play. After the last game of my senior college season, I somehow knew that my body could not be put on the line any longer.

My mindset after the completion of my senior year regarding the NFL was that if they were interested in inviting me to the combine or wanted to come to the University to test me that was great; if not, then I was surprisingly also fine with that. After playing football for 14 seasons, it was time to finally hang up the cleats. That is a decision not so easily made by a lot of football athletes, especially when they are in the NFL and don't know when to say enough is enough. How many surgeries and injuries do you have to sustain until you finally retire? The reason I think some athletes have such a hard time letting go is because of their fear that they have nothing else to fall back on.

Sure, I probably could have played in the CFL or the indoor arena football league after college, but the payout just did not seem to be enough. Why should I risk injury to my neck, back, shoulders and knees for a measly $40,000 to $50,000 a year, when I could use my mind, a bachelor's degree in finance and a minor in Spanish to work up to that amount and beyond in a couple of years? The damage had already been done to my body with all the tackles I had made over the years. I have a neck that likes to crack several times a day, and after my college football career came to an end, I was diagnosed with degenerative disc disease in my lower vertebrae. That would explain my constant lower back pain since I was 18 years old.

Looking back on my decision to stop playing football after college, it was one of the smartest things I have ever done. I enjoy having a high quality of life, and if I had extended my football career, there is no doubt in my mind that I would be far worse off than I am today. Some of the great quarterbacks during my childhood, like Joe Montana, John Elway and Dan Marino are now in the Canton Pro Football Hall of Fame but their bodies paid a terrible price. I would bet you that these quarterbacks have had numerous surgeries related to football injuries, and the game of football has taken away their youthful step for the remainder of their lives. Now their bodies creak and crack when they walk, but if you asked them if it was worth it, I'm sure they would say they would not trade the memories for anything.

That is the double-edged sword with football. On the one hand, it is fun and competitive to play, but on the other hand, your body will ultimately pay the price. There is so much physical contact in the sport that you cannot come away from it without your body being affected in a negative way. With that said, if you asked me if I had to do it all over again would I have played football for 14 seasons? The answer to that question, my friend, would simply be "I would not have changed a thing." Football helped mold me into the person that I am today and in my opinion that is well worth the aches and pains that come along with it.

PUTTING OFF THE WORKING WORLD FOR ONE LAST SUMMER

Once you finally reach your last semester of college without any football responsibilities, it is as refreshing as jumping into an ice tub full of water after a session of doubles. For those who have not gotten to experience this, it is a good thing when your body is overheated and you are drenched in sweat. Sure I was going to miss playing in the games on Saturday afternoons but as far as the practices and meetings were concerned, I was ready to move on. That semester I completed my Bachelor of Science in Finance and also added a Minor in Spanish with a cumulative G.P.A over 3.3. I even took some acting classes that semester and performed in a couple of short plays just for the experience and because I had the time to do it.

I remember one audition that I had for the production of "Taming of the Shrew". I had two monologues memorized from two different contrasting Shakespeare plays as I walked onto the stage. Of course, being the rookie I was, I stumbled through my monologues and pretty much failed miserably. The director was not terribly impressed, but he was interested in hearing one of my impersonations after seeing it on my resume. I told him I could do Sly Stallone from Rocky and he told me that Sly was one of his favorite actors. As I internally prepared myself to shock and awe them I blurted out only two words. You can probably guess what those two words were. I simply said in my best Rocky accent "Yo Adrianne." After a couple of laughs from the people in the stands I proceeded to do an Arnold impersonation from the movie "Pumping Iron." Needless to say, that went over about as well as acting like Rocky Balboa. I wasn't called back for a second audition that day, but it was time to have fun as a regular student for my last semester of college, and I was enjoying it to my fullest.

It was a time of relaxation but also preparation as I started considering where I wanted to work and what I wanted to do when I graduated college. Did I want to work in a place like Boston or what about the financial capital of the world, New York City? The cost of living definitely had to be taken into consideration, not to mention the starting salary. If there is one piece of advice I can give you after you graduate from college, I would highly encourage you to take the summer off before entering the working world. Once you start working you are probably going to get two weeks of vacation a year for your first five years at your job, and your college days will be a distant memory. Use the summer to do something fun like traveling to Europe or working at a part-time job and taking trips to fun destinations around the United States.

Another thing to take into consideration during your last semester is the opportunity you have to study abroad. Did you know that full scholarship players can travel abroad and use their scholarship money to pay for their board, books and tuition? Even if you do not have a scholarship, studying abroad is usually cheaper than if you are going to an out-of-state school. Prior to my final semester, I was considering studying abroad in Seville, Spain. If it had not been for the possibility of playing at the next level, I would have been Spain-bound, and my full scholarship would have covered every bit of it.

The last exam I took before graduating was a Spanish final. I can still remember the exhilaration and sense of accomplishment I felt after my last college exam was complete after five years of college. Many students who saw me after that exam might say that I was skipping and whistling, with a big smile on my face. Although it seemed like a long journey at the time, it surprises me how fast those five years went by. Without a doubt, my personal relationship with Jesus Christ pulled me through college and allowed me to persevere during that experience. It was finally time to make the transition from college student athlete to the working world, but before that would happen, I decided not to start full-time employment until the end of summer.

As job fairs came to Rhode Island, I was seriously considering potential job offers in Boston and New York City. However, the high cost of living was not offset enough by the salary range employers were offering. After graduation, I took a week long excursion with my brother and good friend, Chris DeSimone. It included deep sea fishing and trips to Boston, Newport, Martha's Vineyard, Hoboken and New York City. I stayed in Cleveland during the summer, at my parents' house. Looking to stay busy but still enjoy my last summer, I worked part-time jobs, including personal training at Bally's Total Fitness, security at Jacob's Field for the Cleveland Indian games and personal training for some clients at their home.

It was an enjoyable summer but also a summer of fervent prayer. I prayed to God to bless me with a job that would challenge, fulfill and exceed my expectations. As I sent out resumes to different prospective employers that summer, I received an unexpected call from the Sherwin-Williams Company. This was the same company that I interned with in the Treasury Department at the Corporate Headquarters in downtown Cleveland during the previous summer. That unexpected call would ultimately lead to another answered prayer in my life and send me traveling around the United States and the Caribbean. It also goes to show the importance of gaining practical experience in internships during your time at college. Employers want to hire people they know something about, and internships allow them to gain a comfort level about your work skills. Internships give you an "in" to jobs that would otherwise be very difficult to obtain.

TRAVEL BUG BITES HARD

It was mid-July when I received that unexpected call from the Sherwin-

Williams Company. Earlier that summer, I had inquired about available job openings in the Treasury Department, but there were no openings. The International Treasury Manager, Lee Pena, that took me under his wing during my internship, was kind enough to forward my resume to the other applicable finance related departments in the company. It wasn't long before the Audit Department called for an interview regarding a field auditor position. An interesting twist to your first job out of college might be that it is in a field that you are not totally familiar with. Don't be discouraged if that is your case, because that is where company training comes into play.

It took only one interview with the Audit Department, and later that week, I received the job offer I had been praying for. Sherwin-Williams was flexible with my desire to start after summer, and when it was finally time to go to work, it was a traveler's dream. I was going to train with three different field auditors across the United States. You are probably wondering what I would be training to audit at these different locations. The reason the Sherwin-Williams Company has an internal Audit Department is because there are over 3,000 Sherwin-William Paint Stores located throughout the Unites States. I was not an expert when it came to making or selling paint, but I was eager to learn the business from the ground up.

My first assignment was a two-week trip to Fort Worth, Texas, to meet up with the auditor responsible for the Dallas/Fort Worth audit zone. He would teach me how to audit every aspect of a paint store (including cash control, banking, accounts receivable management, inventory management, financial statements, sales invoices, purchasing and receiving merchandise, store safety, store security controls and staffing). It was a lot of information to take in, but that was why I would be training for six weeks. When I arrived at the Dallas/Fort Worth airport, I remember the auditor telling me how impressed he was that I had reached platinum status due to a certain number of hotel stays with the Hilton Honors program. I didn't think anything of it at the time, but when we drove to our first audit location in south Oklahoma, it was a little surprising to find out that I grabbed the wrong suitcase off the luggage rack. It was definitely a rookie mistake, and the next morning we had to drive back to the airport to return the luggage with the platinum Hilton Honors tag and pick up my suitcase. This was not the best way to make a first impression with your new co-worker.

Training for my first job out of college was pretty intense because I had to absorb so much information in a relatively short period of time. Even though it was challenging, it was exciting to be utilizing my hard-earned bachelor's degree in Finance. It was also fun getting to travel and live on the road. After two weeks in Dallas/Fort Worth, I headed to Hartford, Connecticut, for two weeks with a veteran field auditor. I learned a great deal from him as we traveled to four different paint stores. This time, I made sure to check my luggage tags after I arrived at the airport.

My last two weeks of training took me to San Antonio, Texas, for a two-week period with the auditor of the San Antonio audit zone. I was quickly learning how to conduct a store audit, and by my last two weeks, I was given the lead on the store audits. It was hard to believe how far I had come over six weeks of training. Even though I was burning the midnight oil in using my laptop as I continued to learn the audit program, I knew that this experience would pay off in the long run.

It was an easy decision when it came time to pick which audit zone I wanted to work in after my training was complete. The two choices I had were the Boston audit zone and the St. Louis audit zone. Even though Boston was a big city, the cost of apartments was so expensive that the previous auditor there lived in New Hampshire. Traveling out to the Midwest just seemed like a better fit for me. Before I knew it, my belongings in Cleveland were picked up by the moving company, and I was living in South St. Louis. I was responsible for 50 stores in my audit zone. I went to places like the birthplace of Mark Twain in Hannibal, Missouri, and to the town of Abraham Lincoln in Lincoln, Illinois. My audit zone was considered about 30% travel. I scheduled my audits accordingly, so I would not have to stay on the road over a long period of time.

After working in the St. Louis audit zone for 8 months, the opportunity came to transfer to the Ft. Lauderdale audit zone. This audit zone was perfect for someone who likes beaches and the Caribbean. Getting paid to audit paint stores in places like Key West, Naples, Fort Myers, Miami Beach and Puerto Rico sounded almost too good to be true. I prayed to my personal Savior to send me to Ft. Lauderdale if it was His will. My Field Audit Supervisor at the time helped answer that prayer. This was an excellent opportunity to continue to learn new things in my profession, as I would audit floor covering, intermix and spray equipment facilities. In addition, I would get to practice my Spanish during two-week audit trips to Puerto Rico. Little did I know at the time that I would meet my future wife a little over a month after moving to Ft. Lauderdale.

FINDING TRUE LOVE

As I traveled to Fort Lauderdale in my 1992 Ford Tempo that I nicknamed "Crucificio", I could not help but think of what God had planned for me in South Florida. Of course, there was an exciting new job and different places to visit. The only problem is that you eventually get to a point in your life where you can go to only so many places and see so many things before you want someone special in your life to be part of your adventures. When it came to meeting my future wife for the first time, two places came to my mind. My two preferences were either at church or at a linedance bar. Now I know that seems a little contradictory, but let me first explain. The church is where everyone says you should find a good woman to marry which I attended on a regular basis. The reason I also chose a linedance bar was that I was an avid linedancer and a big fan of country music. I didn't see any harm in meeting a nice lady in a cowgirl hat that shared my same interests.

The first time I met my future wife was at a linedance bar in Davie, Florida, called Davie Junction. I had only been in South Florida for a little over a month; and Cupid shot me with his arrow as soon as I looked into her beautiful eyes. She first spotted me on the dance floor from the second level of the club as she watched me do a little line dancing. That night I was decked out in a pair of carpenter jeans, my black cowboy hat and black alligator boots. After some quality line dancing, I went upstairs to use the restroom. Before I came back downstairs, I briefly stopped behind some people who were facing toward the dance floor. I felt a hand tap me on the shoulder, and a tall gentleman pointed to this young woman sitting on a stool by a table. Little did I know that the tap came from her younger brother who overheard her talking about me to her sister. At the time I wasn't sure exactly what he was implying so I took the opportunity to introduce myself to the young lady and asked her if she would like to two-step. It only took one dance, and I knew that I had to see her again. There was just something different about her (besides her good looks) that aroused my curiosity. Before the night was over, I found her upstairs and asked if it would be all right if I called her sometime to go on a date. Luckily for me, she gave me her cell and home phone that night. I still have those numbers in my wallet six years and one baby boy later.

It took only four months of dating before I proposed to my wife, Tiffany, at the Cleveland Pops Orchestra in downtown Cleveland just before midnight on December 31, 2000. The first time I told Tiffany that I loved her was on an observation tower nestled above the clouds in the tropical rainforest called El Yunque in Puerto Rico. I wanted it to be special, because God blessed me with an angel who would forever change my life and help me grow closer to Him. I also wanted to do the right thing and ask her father's permission for her hand in marriage.

I will never forget the day that Tiffany's father and I played racquetball when he was just starting out in the sport. We played five games and I ended up winning all five. On the way back to their house I decided to ask her father's permission for Tiffany's hand in marriage. Now I admit that I chose the wrong time to ask for permission after not letting him win one racquetball game, and what came next I certainly had coming. After I popped the question to her father, he said, "You beat me in five games of racquetball in a row and did not even let me win one game before asking for my daughter's hand in marriage?" With that aside, he did agree to let me marry his daughter, on the condition we went to marriage counseling classes, which I was more than willing to do. Whenever you pop the question remember that timing unlike mine is everything. We were married the following year on September 22, 2001, and had a beautiful wedding and reception in Key Biscayne, Florida.

Our wedding (like many others during the month of September 2001) did not come without obstacles to overcome. Just eleven days earlier on September 11, 2001, my groomsman and good friend, Chris DeSimone, with whom I played football with at the University of Rhode Island, was tragically killed in the World Trade Center on that horrible day. It was hard to believe what I was seeing on television that Tuesday morning at work because I had just talked to Chris about my wedding the Sunday before. Chris was certainly a good friend who will be truly missed. I'm thankful to know that during our time together at college, I utilized my opportunity to witness to him about my Lord and Savior, Jesus Christ. It really does make all the difference in the world when you lose a loved one but know inside that you answered God's call and shared your spiritual story with them. They may not receive Christ then, but you know that you allowed God to use you to plant a seed which He would hopefully water later in life.

The strong marriage that Tiffany and I enjoy today is entirely a testament to God. He is the glue holding us together. The relationship we each enjoy with our personal Savior, Jesus Christ, is by far the best thing you can have in common with your spouse. The divorce rate in our society is well over 50%, which is a tragedy in itself. When two people unite together in marriage, they are doing it before God. It is a significant commitment to each other for life and not just based on a bunch of feelings. It is a promise to God, and when you get divorced you are breaking that promise. With God, all things are possible, and that is why I believe it is so important to let Him help your marriage flourish and grow.

A GREAT COACH REMEMBERED

It was March 1, 2001 when the most encouraging, caring coach I ever knew went to be with the Lord in heaven. Coach Ray Dorr passed away at the age of 59 after battling Lou Gehrig's disease. Coach Dorr was responsible for recruiting me to the University of Kentucky and never lost sight of my potential on the football field. He took pride in his recruits, and even after the coaching staff got fired at UK, Coach Dorr cared enough to send me a hand-written letter from College Station, Texas, during his new coaching job at Texas A&M. He wrote me to say that he knew I was going to do great things at the University of Kentucky. I can still picture Coach Dorr doing monkey rolls on the football field with the running backs during one of our summer doubles. He had such a zest for life, and it was easy to tell that he was a man filled with the spirit of God. He was a true delight to be around, and it wasn't hard to see he was a bright shining light in a dark world.

Not long after I graduated from the University of Rhode Island I wrote a letter to Coach Dorr. I told him about what I had achieved at the University of Rhode Island and how I gave all the glory and honor to Jesus Christ. I wanted to let Coach Dorr know that his recruit came through just like he said I would. He saw something in me that so many others overlooked and that had a profound impact on my life. Coach Dorr was my mentor, my coach and my good friend. I only wish I could have had the chance to say goodbye. I know that one day I will get to meet him in heaven and that he will have some people like Noah, Abraham, Moses, and most importantly, Jesus, to introduce to me.

I believe that the good Lord used Coach Dorr to work with young student athlete football players and to help them change their lives for the better. I'm sure there are countless stories from former players about his encouraging words and loving heart. He personally motivated me to continue to reach out to young student athletes to help them reach their God-given potential. Coach Dorr coached college football for 33 years, with time spent at Texas A&M, Kentucky, USC, Washington, Kent State and Akron. To show the true spirit of this warrior and champion, I read in an article that during the last year of his life battling his disease, Coach Dorr and his wife, Karen, would lead a weekly Bible study with the quarterbacks he coached at Texas A&M. Coach Dorr will be missed by many, but certainly not forgotten.

MISCONCEPTIONS ABOUT CHRISTIANITY AND POTENTIAL

Is it just me or is there a general misconception that Christians do not know how to enjoy life? The reason I think this misconception exists is because our society defines a good time as getting intoxicated, having promiscuous sex and even doing drugs. That doesn't sound like such a good time to me. I don't think Jesus intended for Christianity to zap us of our zest for life. There should be an unbridled excitement that arises with each new day, because there is a purpose to our very existence. There is a reason you are alive, and God has a purpose for your life. The more time you spent with Jesus in fellowship, the clearer the purpose for your life will become to you.

Regardless of whether you are in high school, college, starting out in the working world or a parent who wants to better understand your children, you have special talents that God has blessed you with. The good Lord would not give you potential if he did not want you to develop it. The reason we were originally created in the Garden of Eden was so God could have fellowship with man and woman. After all, we were created in His image and that is an honor in itself. Although many years have passed from that day in the garden, one timeless thing that remains the same is that God still wants to have fellowship with you. The fact that He sent His Son to die on the cross for us is proof in itself.

When I look back on the past 29 years of my life, I can see God's hand molding and shaping me more and more each day. I'm reminded of the story of Moses when God wanted to use him to lead the Israelites out of Egypt into the Promised Land. You would think that if God personally asked you to do something, it would be difficult to turn him down. When God talked to Moses from the burning bush, it was God's desire and intent to use the 80-year-old Moses to lead the Israelites out of oppression. Instead of Moses jumping onboard from the start, he tells God in Exodus 2:11, "Who am I that I should go to Pharaoh, and that I should bring the children of Israel out of Egypt?" I wonder how many of us say the same thing to ourselves when we feel like God is calling us to do something great. We say, "Lord but who am I?"

Moses goes on to make additional excuses to the Lord about not seeing how people are going to listen to what he has to say and tells God that he is not a very good speaker. God finally gets irritated and angry by Moses' lack of confidence and tells him that He will send his brother, Aaron the Levite, with him and will give Moses the words to put into Aaron's mouth to speak. Even though Moses made all the excuses under the sun of why he was not qualified for such a task, you have to give him credit for eventually taking a step of faith and trusting God. This passage speaks volumes to my life because I have made the same excuses when God has called me to do something for His kingdom. In the past, I have questioned what difference I could make in peoples lives and lost sight of the fact that the Creator of the Universe was on my side.

If God only used people who were qualified to do His work, there would be a nonexistent list, because everyone falls short of the glory of God except Jesus Christ. The truth is that God takes unqualified people who have problems of varying degrees in their lives and completely turns them around and makes them qualified. It is the power of His mercy and grace that allows us to exceed other people's expectations and achieve our God-given potential because of a personal relationship with Jesus Christ. The same Moses who was so uncertain of what difference he could make can be found later in Numbers 14:19, pleading with God to spare his people for their sins and to forgive them. That is quite a transformation, and the amazing thing is that God listened to Moses and spared the Israelites that day.

FINDING HAPPINESS AND PROTECTION IN THE LORD

The world we live in tries to give us a million different ways to find happiness in life apart from God. There are things we can do and accomplish that will make us content for a short period of time, but before long, we will be hungry once again. If there was ever a King who had it all in life it was King Solomon. He was richer than all the mighty Kings combined before and after him. This was a King who indulged in all the pleasures imaginable, and in the end his futile attempt for happiness apart from God led to this very conclusion: King Solomon realized that nothing on this earth could ever fill the void in his heart except the God who created him. This is probably the most valuable lesson we can ever learn in life. Life is too short not to learn from other peoples mistakes. Don't forget that besides King Solomon's being the wealthiest man around, he was also the wisest, thanks to God's blessings. This was a person who knew exactly what he was talking about, due to his experiences with self indulgence.

The only way to fill that void in your heart for good is to receive Jesus Christ as your personal Savior. People try and try again to do things their own way and end up falling flat on their faces. Don't you think it is time we give God control of our lives? Instead of being the co-pilot of this life of ours, we need to get in the backseat, and let God do the driving. He knows what is best for us, but we have to trust Him. We should seek Him with all our heart and strive to have the same faith that King David had in God. When David went to kill Goliath that day on the field of battle, he knew he only needed one stone to slay the giant. Some might ask why he had more than one smooth stone in his pouch as he went to battle for the Lord. The extra stones were not there in case he missed Goliath the first time. This extraordinary man of faith had just enough stones to take care of Goliath and his brothers if they decided to join in from the crowd. King David was known as a man after God's heart. No one knows your heart and inner desires better than the Lord. Is your heart focusing on things of this world or on God's plan for your life?

As we move forward and encounter temptations in this world, we have the opportunity to put on the whole armor of God to protect us. I have always compared it to suiting up for a football game, but this is armor not easily seen by the naked eye. In Ephesians 6:11 it says, "Put on the whole armor of God, that you may be able to stand against the wiles of the devil." The Lord wants to protect us from the evil one and in Ephesians 6:14-17 Paul tells us how when he says,

Stand therefore, having girded your waist with truth, having put on the breastplate of righteousness, and having shod your feet with the preparation of the gospel of peace; above all, taking the shield of faith with which you will be able to quench all the fiery darts of the wicked one. And take the helmet of salvation, and the sword of the Spirit, which is the word of God;"

Paul is telling us that the overall importance of walking daily with Jesus Christ is not to overcome some of the temptation that comes our way but all of it. Christians are no longer slaves to sin due to putting off the old and taking on the new. If the armor of God is used correctly, we are firmly protected from temptation in our lives. I know it is easier said than done but that is why I think Paul goes on to talk about the significance of praying through the Holy Spirit and reaching out to God with all your heart. Understanding and applying the word of God in your life is the weapon we have to fight back. When Jesus was tempted for 40 days and 40 nights, He used the sword of the Spirit every time to resist Satan, and so can you.

MAKING A HOME IN NORTH CAROLINA

If there was ever a place that I could have envisioned myself living in until the Lord takes me home, that place would be North Carolina. I like to call it the land of milk and honey, the headquarters of the Bible belt and the true source of sweet home Southern hospitality. It was July 2001, and life on the road as a traveling auditor was finally starting to take a toll on me after two years. I enjoyed getting to audit stores in places that people usually went for vacation, but being an auditor is not exactly a job that allows you to build a lot of camaraderie with your fellow co-workers. There is a new store to audit every 3 to 4 days and when you walk in the front door at seven in the morning, a store manager is not likely to welcome you with open arms.

Auditing was a great experience to learn about the all-encompassing operations of a paint store, but I was ready to move on to something new and exciting. The opportunity came in July when an Accounting position opened up at a Sherwin-Williams manufacturing facility in Greensboro, North Carolina. I discussed the open position with my future wife, Tiffany, and she encouraged me to interview for the position. Once again I prayed to God that if it was His will for us to move, to let the transition be a smooth one. Sure enough, God answered my prayer, as a phone interview led to a personal interview in Greensboro. Two days after I flew back to Florida, I received a job offer over the phone.

Since that initial long 12-hour drive from Pembroke Pines, Florida to Greensboro, NC, my family is going on its fifth year in North Carolina. I cannot think of another place in the world that I would rather live and raise a family. You are a hop, jump and skip away from the mountains and the ocean is about three and a half hours away. The Lord continues to work in my life to help me develop my potential through personal time spent with Him and the fellowship my family enjoys at Friendly Avenue Baptist Church. It feels like Jesus has something big planned for me just over the horizon, and I am looking forward to watching it unfold before my eyes.

In October 2004 I left the Sherwin-Williams Company to work as an Accountant at the Deere-Hitachi Construction and Machinery Corporation where we are the main producer of mid-size excavators in North America. I thank God every day for helping me stay focused in college to obtain my bachelor's degree in finance, as the long hours I put in studying are now paying off in big dividends. They say hindsight is always 20/20, but when you can hear a story from a person who has been in your shoes, maybe it hits home a little sooner.

In less than a month I'll turn 30 years old and in some eyes be considered what they call "Over the Hill." My playing days on the football field are a distant memory, but thanks to Jesus it feels like my life has just begun. As each new year passes, I plan to age like a fine wine. At 30 years old I'll be publishing my first book, later in the year enter my first bodybuilding competition since I was in my teens, and most importantly, my wife and I will be having our second child together. Inside I still feel the youthful spirit of that child who wanted to tackle everything in sight. It is kind of ironic that instead of tackling people now, I am more determined than ever to tackle God's plan for my life. There is a great deal to be accomplished for God's kingdom, and it is my desire to focus on the Christian student athletes of tomorrow.

I'm focused more than ever on pressing toward the goal of spending eternity in heaven with Jesus Christ. I have had the opportunity to meet my childhood movie hero, Arnold Swartzenegger, and recently, President George Bush, but I know that both are going to fail in comparison to meeting Jesus Christ in heaven. Before my time comes, I want to say I did everything I could to partake in the Great Commission. I want to be able to stand before the Father and hear Him say "Good job, my faithful servant." There is a place waiting for me in heaven like I have never seen before and that day will be glorious indeed! I know that in this life I am going to stumble and fall, but the important thing is that I keep getting back up. Never quitting and always staying in pursuit of seeing this world through the eyes of Christ will help me become a better disciple. It will make me a better witness as I share my story with others about how my personal Savior, Jesus Christ, touched and changed my life.

I hope this book gave you some insight about making the most of your life and enjoying every moment. Learning to grow closer to Jesus is an exciting adventure, and if you pay attention to the details in your life, you will see where He is leading you. He has great things planned for you and if you take a step of faith in answering your God-given call, life will be more fulfilling than you ever could have imagined. In Mark 10:45 Jesus says, "For even the Son of Man did not come to be served, but to serve, and to give His life a ransom for many." I wonder how faithful you have been in serving God instead of being served. If the Son of God came as a sacrifice for us, how much more should we put ourselves on the line for Him?

I encourage you to walk on higher ground as you travel down your path in life. Don't get caught up in building treasures on earth but rather lay your treasures up in heaven by answering God's call for your life. As your good works and faithfulness multiply your crowns in heaven, you will be setting yourself apart from what has been considered the selfish norm in our society for far too long. Good role models for our younger generation are hard to come by these days, but I know that you are up for the challenge. After all, you could be the athlete on the poster hanging in my son's room when he gets older. Jesus never said it was going to be easy, but rest assured, my brothers and sisters, the trip to heaven will make it all worth it. Awaken the spirit within and let's soar to new heights together.

NOTES

Chapter 1: The Dream of a Young Child
1. Reprinted by permission. *Wild at Heart*, John Eldridge, 2001, Thomas Nelson Inc., Nashville, Tennessee. All rights reserved.
2. Reprinted by permission. *The Decline of Males*, Lionel Tigers, 1999, St. Martin's Press, New York, New York. All rights reserved.

Chapter 2: The Anticipated Recruiting Process
1. Proverbs 19:21.
2. Philippians 4:6-7.

Chapter 3: First Semester at College
1. Matthew 5:16.
2. 1 John 4:4.
3. National Center for Education Statistics (NCES), Condition of Education 2004.
4. Statistics and facts used from the NFLPA website. By permission of the NFLPA.

Chapter 4: Juggling Academics, Athletics and a Social Life
1. Matthew 13:37.
2. 1997 Edition of the University of Kentucky Football Media Guide.

Chapter 5: The Biggest Decision You'll Ever Make
1. John 3:16.
2. 2 Corinthians 5:17.
3. John 8:12.
4. Ephesians 2:8-9.
5. Romans 10:9-10.
6. Matthew 12:31.
7. Reprinted by permission. *Unto the Hills*, Billy Graham, 1996, W. Publishing, a division of Thomas Nelson, Inc., Nashville, Tennessee. All rights reserved.
8. Romans 10:12-13.

9. Romans 3:23.
10. Romans 6:23.
11. 1 John 1:9.
12. John 20:27.
13. John 20:28.
14. John 20:29.
15. Acts 9:1-2.
16. Acts 9:3.
17. Acts 9:4.
18. 2 Corinthians 12:9.
19. 1 Corinthians 3:16.
20. Philippians 4:13.
21. Psalm 23:1-4.
22. Matthew 10:30-31.
23. Job 1:20.
24. Job 1:21.

Chapter 6: Should I Stay, or Should I Go?
1. Matthew 7:7.
2. Hebrews 13:8.
3. 2 Chronicles 1:7.
4. 2 Chronicles 1:9.
5. 2 Chronicles 1:11-12.
6. Matthew 9:11.
7. Matthew 9:12-13.

Chapter 7: You're Only as Good as You Think You Are
1. Psalm 37:4.
2. Teddy Roosevelt quotation. By permission of the Theodore Roosevelt Association.
3. Matthew 4:10.
4. 2 Timothy 3:16.
5. Exodus 16:35.
6. Exodus 24:18.
7. Exodus 34:28.
8. Numbers 13:25.
9. Numbers 14:33-34.

10. 1 Samuel 17:16.
11. Acts 1:3.
12. Teddy Roosevelt quotation. By permission of the Theodore Roosevelt Association.

Chapter 8: Life Beyond College Athletics
1. 1 Corinthians 13:11.
2. Jeremiah 17:10.
3. Exodus 2:11.
4. Ephesians 6:11.
5. Ephesians 6:14-17.
6. Mark 10:45.

ABOUT THE AUTHOR

Miguel Viera, his wife, Tiffany, and son, Mason, currently live in Jamestown, NC. He works at the Deere Hitachi Construction Machinery Corporation as an Accountant. The family attends Friendly Avenue Baptist Church where Miguel is a Deacon, Co-Teacher of the Homebuilders Sunday School class and involved with the Greensboro Jail Ministry.

The creation of this book has led Miguel to start a new ministry called "Playing for Jesus Ministries." This ministry is focused on unleashing the power of student athletes on and off the playing field one Christian at a time. This will be accomplished through a monthly newsletter distributed via email that offers biblical insight for Christian living and also gives student athletes the opportunity to share their accomplishments through Jesus on the playing field. If you would like to receive this newsletter or share an encouraging story about your sport, please email us at viera40@msn.com or visit www.myspace.com/viera40.

Miguel is available for motivational speaking engagements at churches, high schools and colleges upon request. His hopes for the distribution of this book are to solely spread the gospel of Jesus Christ and revitalize the significant importance of positive role models for our younger generation through Christian student athletes.

If you enjoyed reading this book and it has changed your life in some way, we would love to hear about your story. I hope you made the decision to receive Jesus as the Lord of your life. It is the biggest decision you can ever make and one I promise you will never regret. One day spent with Jesus Christ is far better than a lifetime spent without Him.

ISBN 1412086191-1